speed Cleaning 101

Cut your cleaning time in half!

Meredith® Books
Des Moines, Iowa

Speed Cleaning 101

Writer: Laura Dellutri
Editor: Paula Marshall
Project Manager: Cathy Long
Contributing Editor: Diane Witosky
Graphic Designer: Matthew Eberhart
Copy Chief: Terri Fredrickson
Publishing Operations Manager: Karen Schirm
Edit and Design Production Coordinator: Mary Lee Gavin
Editorial Assistants: Kaye Chabot, Kairee Windsor
Marketing Product Managers: Aparna Pande, Isaac Petersen,
    Gina Rickert, Stephen Rogers, Brent Wiersma, Tyler Woods
Book Production Managers: Pam Kvitne, Marjorie J. Schenkelberg, Rick von Holdt, Mark Weaver
Contributing Copy Editor: Joyce Gemperlein
Contributing Proofreaders: Sherry Hames, Gretchen Kauffman, Jody Speer
Cover Photographer: Andy Lyons
Contributing Illustrator: Tina Vey
Indexer: Kathleen Poole

Meredith₀ Books

Executive Director, Editorial: Gregory H. Kayko
Executive Director, Design: Matt Strelecki
Executive Editor/Group Manager: Denise Caringer

Publisher and Editor in Chief: James D. Blume
Editorial Director: Linda Raglan Cunningham
Executive Director, Marketing: Jeffrey B. Myers
Executive Director, New Business Development: Todd M. Davis
Executive Director, Sales: Ken Zagor
Director, Operations: George A. Susral
Director, Production: Douglas M. Johnston
Business Director: Jim Leonard

Vice President and General Manager: Douglas J. Guendel

Meredith Publishing Group

President: Jack Griffin
Senior Vice President: Bob Mate

Meredith Corporation

Chairman and Chief Executive Officer: William T. Kerr
President and Chief Operating Officer: Stephen M. Lacy

In Memoriam: E.T. Meredith III (1933-2003)

All of us at Meredith® Books are dedicated to providing you with information and ideas to enhance your home. We welcome your comments and suggestions. Write to us at: Meredith Books, Home Design and Care Editorial Department, 1716 Locust St., Des Moines, IA 50309-3023.

If you would like to purchase any of our home design and care, cooking, decorating, gardening, or home improvement books, check wherever quality books are sold. Or visit us at: meredithbooks.com

Note to Readers: Due to differing conditions, tools, and individual skills, Meredith Corporation and The Healthy Housekeeper, Inc., assume no responsibility for any damages, injuries suffered, or losses incurred as a result of following the information published in this book. Always read and observe all of the safety precautions provided by manufacturers, and follow all accepted safety procedures.

About the Author

Laura Dellutri, "The Healthy Housekeeper," is a mom, cleaning expert, speed-cleaning consultant, entrepreneur, owner of a professional janitorial firm, author, and radio and television personality.

Her Cinderella story began in 1990 when she started a residential cleaning company, House Cleaning Services. Dismayed with conventional cleaning myths and techniques, she developed her own style of cleaning that helped her start a commercial janitorial business, America's Cleaning Connection, in 1994. Ms. Dellutri has also developed training and certification programs for the commercial janitorial industry and professional residential maid services that have been used worldwide.

In 1994, her TV segments started when she was invited to be a regular weekly guest on CBS television affiliate KMTV 3. Her popularity grew and she was asked to be a guest on the home-show circuit and was interviewed by several large-city newspapers and national magazines. Now, Ms. Dellutri travels the United States appearing on television shows from New York to Los Angeles. She has appeared on popular national shows including *ABC's The View, Living it Up with Jack and Ali* and *Soap Talk.* She has appeared on the Style Network, FOX, NBC, CBS, WB, ABC, and HGTV. She also appears at home-and-garden shows, women's conventions, and is often quoted in magazines and newspapers nationwide, including *Woman's Day, Lifetime Magazine, New York Daily News, And Reader's Digest* among others.

*For more information about The Healthy Housekeeper
visit her website www.healthyhousekeeper.com*

Acknowledgements
Many thanks to God first. My husband and five children. My dear mother, Barbara, who made me clean growing up. My six siblings who encourage me. All the wonderful people that helped me along the way: Meredith Books, family members, church friends, new and old friends, Brian Santos—The Wall Wizard, and business colleagues.
God bless you all for your acts of kindness!

Table of Contents

Introduction 5

CHAPTER ONE
Get Ready to Speed Clean! 8

CHAPTER TWO
Getting in the Mood to Clean 46

CHAPTER THREE
Speed Cleaning Techniques of the Pros 58

CHAPTER FOUR
Your Pro Cleaning Kit 68

CHAPTER FIVE
Wet and Dry Work .88

CHAPTER SIX
Speed Cleaning Room by Room 100

CHAPTER SEVEN
Speed Clean Your Laundry Room 120

CHAPTER EIGHT
Organization 140

Glossary 186

Laura's Favorite Products 188

Index 190

Speed Cleaning 101

INTRODUCTION

Many domestic arguments among men, women, and children have started over cleaning chores. Disputes can erupt over who should be doing the work, how often, and when. Women want more help around the house. Men want the women to quit stressing about the whole cleaning thing. Children want to do as little cleaning as possible; they'd rather run off and play. Cleaning is a hot topic because our homes get dirty every single day.

Just mention the word "cleaning" in your workplace. Everyone has advice to give or a problem he or she struggles with. The biggest complaint I hear is that people can't find the time in today's fast-paced society to clean their homes. Let's face it, we are all trying to find time, make more time, or just be on time. If I could sum up in one word what this book can give you, it would be TIME. By following these tips, you'll find you have more time to do the things you enjoy and more time for family, while spending less time cleaning the house!

There is something enticing and uplifting about a clean home. It gives us a sense of accomplishment and makes a statement about how we control our home environments. We decorate our homes as a reflection of our personal style and individual taste. Part of our style includes our standard of cleaning. We can feel overwhelmed and stressed when our homes are out of control; so, too, we can relax when they are clean and orderly.

If you don't make cleaning your home a priority, you are one of those people who do not stress over cleaning. Instead, you choose to prioritize your life with more pressing matters. It is perfectly fine to do that too. This book helps both the cleaning fanatic and the cleaning dramatic—the "I hate to clean and my life is a shambles" person. This book is designed to help everyone clean easier, faster, and better than ever before.

Scrubbing away day after day in my residential-cleaning business took time and energy. My clients referred to me as a "cleaning tornado" because I was able to work in four homes in one day. I admit there were times I felt like Cinderella left at home to do the cleaning while everyone else went to the ball. But even on those Cinderella days, deep down inside, I knew that when the client walked in the door—kids in tow after a long hectic workday—she could at least know she was walking into a clean home. Our homes are our castles, a refuge from the pressures of everyday life. My clients' joy motivated me to clean.

My numerous housecleaning experiences coupled with my clients' kindnesses encouraged me to clean more houses faster, to keep on the prowl for better cleaning tools, and to become the Speed Cleaning whiz I am today!

For those of you who are thinking, "Not me! I could never feel motivated. I hate to clean. My house is a wreck, but I know where everything is, so let's leave well enough alone!" I say, GREAT! Some of my best clients' homes were the most disorganized places you could ever imagine. It's OK to have a messy home. Some of the most loving, balanced, and least-stressed people I have ever met lived in homes that were a "mess."

What is my philosophy on cleaning? In the scheme of life, who really cares about having a spotlessly clean home? Life—with its children, pets, and fun—is messy. We only need to clean up for health, image, and a sense of well-being. Most important, our homes are a place to live, love, relax, and enjoy life.

Then why the need for this book? I am here to make your life easier and less stressful and to help you find more time in your day. Consider me the busy person's hero who just wants you to enjoy life a little bit more!

Ahh, I know it all sounds too good to be true. You can get your housecleaning done in half the time, freeing up time for you to enjoy the more important things in life. Does it mean that you are cutting corners and not properly cleaning and disinfecting your home? No, absolutely not! This book will teach you how to "clean smarter, not harder." It's like learning to type. At first you peck away at the keyboard, but then you learn the correct technique. Before you know it, you're typing faster and faster. You pick up speed each time you do the task. Cleaning is no different. Once you learn the proper techniques, you can clean your home in half the time.

What will this book teach you? You'll learn cleaning tips that the professionals use. As you begin to follow these simple techniques, you'll find the work becoming easier and easier. You will also be able to analyze a cleaning job and work smarter, not harder. So sit back and relax as you learn the professional techniques, the quickest methods, and the best tools. It can be easy if you know the professional way to do it.

For more information about Speed Cleaning or about me, The Healthy Housekeeper, visit my website at *www.healthyhousekeeper.com.*

The Healthy Housekeeper

Laura Dellutri

CHAPTER ONE

Get Ready to Speed Clean!

If you're tired of feeling guilty and stressed because you don't have time to do all the cleaning you would like to—RELAX! My experience cleaning thousands of homes has truly made me the "speed-cleaning queen" of the 21st century.

Learning to clean properly and efficiently is as important as learning how to balance a checkbook. It's something we all have to do, and doing it right saves a lot of time and headaches. By learning the right way to clean, not only will you clean your home more thoroughly, you will clean your home much faster too. By the end of this book, you'll be Speed Cleaning with the best of them.

This book contains speed-cleaning techniques that have been tested in the professional cleaning industry. I learned most of them in residential homes and commercial buildings after cleaning those hundreds of times. I also have developed a complete employee-training system that has been used worldwide in the commercial janitorial business. The results are phenomenal.

This book also is inspired in part by the methods my husband and I are using to teach our five children—by the time they are 16 years old—some of the skills they will need when they are managing their own homes. They'll need to know how to clean a toilet, load a dishwasher, dust, do laundry, iron, and cook meals.

Speed Cleaning has three basic components. Following them may involve changing your habits and mind-set about how to clean. You'll have to throw out the old-fashioned ideas and processes that take all day to complete (we will discuss those throughout the book). Then, you can start with a fresh attitude about cleaning your home in this whole new way.

The Three Ts: Tools • Techniques • Time

Each component is necessary to the success of your cleaning strategy, and they work together. It's a simple concept once you have the Three Ts in place.

Tools

Analyze your cleaning tools. Which tool for each job is the safest, fastest, and easiest to use? Finding the right tools is one of the speed-cleaning secrets.

★ Buy a long-handled ceiling fan brush from a home center or hardware store (about $10) and you'll be able to clean each ceiling fan in your home in about 2 minutes. Without the brush, you'll need to climb a ladder and spend 8 to 10 minutes per fan to do the job.

★ Don't waste time (up to 20 minutes) cleaning the kitchen floor with a 7-inch, bacteria-infested sponge mop when you can use a 15-inch microfiber flat mop to do a healthier job in just 5 minutes.

Once you evaluate the tools you're using, you'll find plenty of affordable cleaning tools that can do the work for you.

Techniques

The way you move through a room, the direction your hands move to wipe an area—even the way you spray cleaning chemicals on a surface—are important considerations.

★ Overspraying cleaning products on surfaces causes buildup and requires unnecessary work to remove the excess.

★ Wiping in a circular motion takes longer than wiping in horizontal overlapping strokes.

Who would have thought these simple things could make such a big difference?

Time

Taking a few minutes to analyze the job in its entirety saves you time in the end because you'll find you are working more efficiently. Before starting a cleaning task, ask these questions.

★ How long should it take?
★ What do you need to do to make the task easier and faster?
★ What is the most efficient traffic pattern?

Experience shows that if you know the time involved to complete a task—for example, mopping the kitchen floor should take 5 minutes—you are more apt to do the task because you can justify finding the time in your busy schedule or daily routine.

TIP Speed Cleaning is a whole new way of cleaning your home. You can apply the Speed Cleaning concept in all types of dwellings: homes, apartments, condominiums, and even mansions. The basic premise is the same; the techniques vary little as you travel from room to room.

21st-Century Cleaning Terms

It's important to understand the basic cleaning terms so you'll know if you are overcleaning, undercleaning, or just plain need to do some cleaning!

Most professional cleaning companies understand the lingo associated with household cleaning tasks, but most regular folks don't. Let's face it: The only school of cleaning we've attended has been taught by our parents. (Some schools still teach home economics, but who really taught most of us the basics?) How many parents talked about cleaning tools, cleaning schedules, and cleaning techniques?

In this section you'll find definitions of types of cleaning, such as Daily Cleaning, Basic Cleaning, Seasonal Cleaning, Spruce-Up Cleaning, Cosmetic Cleaning, and Preventive Cleaning. These sections explain how often each should be done in your home and how to encourage family members to pitch in to help.

Daily Cleaning

Daily Cleaning consists of the routine daily chores we have to do just to keep a home tidy. These tasks are

★ Wash the dishes   ★ Make the beds   ★ Sort junk mail
★ Do the laundry   ★ Pick up clothes
★ Pick up the things that get strewn about the house during an average day.

You can also keep your home tidy by using the following Speed Cleaning 101 Quick Tips:

Quick Tips

Use mats to keep the dirt out. Start at the entrance. Eighty-five percent of the dirt that comes into your home comes in on the bottom of shoes. Placing mats and wiping shoes on them 6 to 8 times before entering your home will remove about 80 percent of the dirt. Sturdy mats can be bought at most home centers.

Choose mats that will clean the bottom of shoes aggressively. High-quality artificial turf mats have 35,000 active scraper blades per mat. These mats are configured so that just walking will effectively clean the bottom of shoes, keeping the dirt out of your home. Choose commercial grade, vinyl-backed indoor mats that can reduce falls and trap loose dirt. And don't forget to put a mat by the door from the garage if your family uses that entry.

Start a NO SHOE rule. If you want to remove 85 percent of the dirt that gets into your home, don't let anyone wear shoes indoors. Have a basket or shoe shelf and a bench or chair for people to sit on and remove their shoes as they enter. A seat will make taking off shoes more user-friendly and comfortable. By making taking off shoes comfortable, you streamline the process and reduce the number of complaints you will hear when enforcing your NO SHOE rule.

Create a place to put coats, backpacks, and briefcases. If your home has an attached garage, hang a shelf and hooks in it for shoes, coats, backpacks, and briefcases to help keep all those items in one organized place instead of strewn throughout your house. Once my children hit the door, chaos hits the home. Backpacks get tossed, shoes fly off, and jackets fall to the ground. I put a stop to that fast by giving them a place to put their stuff. You also can use plastic drawer units on wheels or bins in the garage. Hats, gloves, scarves, and other items can be placed in these to stop the insanity of looking for a lost mitten on a day that has a 30-degree-below-zero wind chill. Even your 3-year-old's lost shoe can wreak havoc when you're trying to get to preschool on time!

Clear the clutter daily with one basket. Buy one 10-inch plastic tub or woven basket that's designated as the daily basket. Use this as the catchall for papers that come into the house each day. The goal is to sift through the basket every day. This way you'll easily be able to deal with the flyer for the school bake sale, the homework assignment that needs a signature, your spouse's ATM receipt that needs to be recorded in the checkbook, and the business card you need to file. Even the day's mail can go in there until you have a moment to sort it. Just use one daily basket. If you don't have the time to go through it each day, you, your children, and spouse know that an item is in the daily basket—not misplaced—avoiding household drama.

Assign children a 10-minute "pickup time" each morning. Teach them to use this time to put away toys, pick up whatever is scattered on the floors, and make beds. When those three areas are in disarray, a child's room looks like a disaster zone. This tip, consistently enforced, can become a habit like teaching your children to brush their teeth. And it eliminates the "disaster zone" phenomenon you have to deal with every weekend.

Have everyone in the home make the beds daily. Having the bed made gives the entire bedroom a neat appearance. It's easier for parents who consistently make their own bed to get their children to make their beds. After all, children learn what they live and see. Remember, you are the children's cleaning role models: If you complain about cleaning, chances are they will complain about cleaning. (What about children who consistently will not make their beds? We will answer that question in the next section.)

Establish Cleaning Boundaries

Just how clean should your home be? How much work should your children do in the home? How hard should you push your family when it comes to maintaining standards of cleaning in your home? To answer these questions—and before you become an accomplished Speed Cleaner—you need to establish your cleaning boundaries. This boundary is the level of clean that's acceptable to you and your family. You clean to that level only—but setting the boundary commits you to consistently cleaning your home to that level.

These boundaries are flexible—what works for the first five years of raising your family likely will change in the next five. You may have to compromise along the way as your children reach different ages or your job changes. Your family's needs, health issues, and other factors can influence how much time and energy you put into cleaning. The most important thing is to be flexible instead of being so rigid in your cleaning boundaries that you stress out yourself or your family. Treat your cleaning boundaries as a goal, not an obsession.

When establishing boundaries, it all comes down to what you will accept. Forget about what other people think, do, or say. You run your household; they don't! Your cleaning standard is yours alone to set. So if you want set your cleaning boundaries high—such as hospital clean—or low—such as a teenager's room that's a complete mess—go ahead!

Here are some thoughts on cleaning boundaries from people I know.

An entrepreneurial mother who owns a sandwich franchise restaurant along with her husband told me, "I will have a clean house again someday, as soon as my five children are grown."

> **Cleaning boundary established** She's made a decision not to stress about the mess of five children and has a vision of when she'll have the clean home she wants—after the kids are grown and out of the home. She has a realistic cleaning boundary for her family and has decided to accept the fact that her house won't be perfectly clean at this time in her life.

My own mother said, "Why should I ever purchase a dishwasher? I have seven dishwashers living in my home!"

> **Cleaning boundary established** Mom told us loud and clear that she was not the maid in our home. All of us children knew it was our responsibility to help with the cleaning chores in the home.

My friend who just had a baby said, "I used to keep our home spotless when we were first married, but since the baby was born, the shelves are dustier and the house looks a little more cluttered. I don't mind. It's more important to enjoy spending time holding my baby, just snuggling with her. Before I know it, she will be outside playing with all the kids, growing up too quickly."

> **Cleaning boundary established** Her boundary was clear, her cleaning priorities and time requirements shifted to taking care of baby, and she was not going to worry about feeling guilty about some dust on the shelf.

So how do you establish boundaries in your home? Decide what level of cleaning you can live with on a daily basis. Ask yourself some questions.

★ Are you the type of person who wants a meticulous home where you can "eat off the floor"?

★ Do you want to keep the house clean, sanitized, and organized so that you can walk in and feel comforted by your home's environment?

★ Do you just need a clear path into the kitchen, bathroom, and bedroom?

The choice is yours!

RATE YOUR STANDARD OF HOME CLEANING

Determine the exact standard of clean you want based on the cleaning level you already have. Choose the number from the list below that best reflects your cleaning standard, with 1 being the lowest cleaning level and 10 the highest.

1. Cleaning is non-existent in the home. It has not been cleaned in years.
2. Cleaning is done once or twice a year.
3. Cleaning is done every few months.
4. Cleaning is done about once a month.
5. Cleaning is done as needed, depending on number of children, people, and pets in the home. This could vary.
6. Cleaning is done two times per month.
7. Cleaning is done three times per month.
8. Cleaning is done weekly.
9. Cleaning is done two to three times per week.
10. Cleaning is done daily.

Once you determine what your cleaning standard is, it becomes easy to establish your cleaning boundaries—it's simply a matter of how clean you want your home to be. My standard when all the children were at home was number 8. We had to clean weekly because everything got dirty fast with five children in the house. If we did not clean the bathrooms, vacuum, and dust on this schedule, things would get out of control and make the whole house look messy.

Now we have three children graduated from school and out of the home. Because we now have three fewer people living in the home, there is less wear and tear, and the house stays cleaner longer! Now I have relaxed my standard of cleaning to a 7. Of course, when company comes, I jump my standard to a 10! Again, keep in mind that there will be times when you will need to adjust your standard based on situations that arise. Be flexible, but be aware of what you need to do to satisfy the standard you have set.

Set Children's Cleaning Boundaries Too

When it comes to children and setting a cleaning boundary, consistency is important. The best plan of action is to establish cleaning boundaries with your children when they are as young as possible. Most 2- and 3-year-olds can pick up their toys, and they can be great helpers.

Rule No. 1 *Never clean up after your children after the age of 3, or you will find yourself feeling like their personal maid in no time!*

Starting a child young with cleaning boundaries will save you many stressful days when he or she is a teenager. The goal is to dole out age-appropriate tasks as the children mature. With my children, I have three key cleaning boundaries:

1. The children clean up any messes they make.
2. The children maintain fairly clean and organized bedrooms.
3. The children do their fair share of household chores.

I have five children. Everyone has to chip in and help with the housecleaning chores. My children know what the boundaries are, and we work hard on consistently enforcing them. Expect your children to push, plead, procrastinate, and make endless empty promises to get out of cleaning.

Do you have to be a drill sergeant, never deviating from your cleaning standards for your children? When my son broke his leg, of course we didn't ride him about the condition of his room. There have been other times when my children had important events and did not have the time to clean. In special cases, we may have released their cleaning responsibilities that day. We enforced our boundaries very consistently over the years, but we were not so rigid that the children felt like they lived with a drill sergeant.

Will your kids be perfect with the cleaning chores? Realistically speaking, absolutely not! They are kids. Even as adults we can be lazy and try to get out of work at times. It's best to expect your children to feel the same way.

True Cleaning Confessions

Many parents stress out over the condition of their children's bedrooms. With the law of averages and my own five children to raise, it was inevitable that at least one of my children was going to be domestically challenged when it came to room cleaning and daily bed making. That's when I learned firsthand how boundaries may not work with some children.

My husband and I felt terrible because our daughter's room from age 14 was horrific. We felt like failures as parents: That girl simply would not keep her room clean. She had the skills to do the cleaning because she worked for our janitorial company starting at age 15 and was professionally trained to clean. My husband and I tried grounding her and taking away privileges to no avail. She would clean the room after we threatened bodily harm (just kidding). It would take her all day long—8 to 10 hours—to clean a 12×15-foot room. Two hours after cleaning, the bedroom would be a total wreck again. She could not and would not get the cleaning thing together. After many tense days, we took the focus off the cleaning and switched our priorities to focus on her.

Taking the advice of a friend who's a family counselor, we closed the door to the bedroom. We did not let guests see her room. We did not enter the disaster zone. Once we backed off the power struggle over the bedroom, we were able to shift our focus to more pressing parental matters, such as preparing her for college and opening up her first checking account. As soon as we shifted our focus and priorities, so did she. She focused on the big picture of her life: graduating from high school and becoming an adult. She decided to graduate a year early and met with her counselor to formulate a plan. Much to our surprise, our daughter with the messy room graduated from high school a year early and started college that fall.

The point Don't stick with a plan that isn't working! If you run into a brick wall and find that some of your cleaning boundaries don't work, come up with a new plan of action. Take some time to refocus your priorities.

Basic Cleaning

Basic Cleaning consists of the chores that need to be done on a regular basis just to maintain the cleanliness level in your home. Basic Cleaning is not the same as doing the Daily Cleaning chores, but it is a necessary step to establish a baseline that can be maintained by Speed Cleaning.

Basic Cleaning includes vacuuming, dusting, disinfecting the bathrooms, removing the trash, and washing all the hard-surface floors. Most maid services sell a "basic cleaning package," which they recommend if they are going to come to your house regularly. This package would normally consist of

- ★ Vacuuming carpets
- ★ Vacuuming stairs
- ★ Vacuuming furniture
- ★ Dusting furniture
- ★ Vacuuming hard floors
- ★ Removing cobwebs
- ★ Dusting windowsills and landings
- ★ Dusting wall hangings
- ★ Picking up and straightening pillows and magazines
- ★ Cleaning the entry and patio doors
- ★ Cleaning and disinfecting the bathrooms
- ★ Making the beds and changing the linens
- ★ Changing towels
- ★ Cleaning kitchen floors and sinks and spot-cleaning cabinets
- ★ Cleaning kitchen counters and the outsides of the appliances
- ★ Cleaning the inside of the microwave
- ★ Spot-cleaning walls
- ★ Emptying the trash

This list really has no surprises. Many of these tasks may already be a part of your cleaning routine. The question that you may want answered is *"How often do I really have to do this?"*

To determine the answer to this big question, review your answers to the rating of your cleaning standard. Do you want to be an 8 on the cleaning scale? That requires once-a-week cleaning. Or do you lack the time to clean and are you willing to compromise on a mid-range 5 standard?

Other questions to consider as you do your Basic Cleaning include
★ Are you a neat freak?
★ Are you, or another household member, a "walking mess maker"?
★ Do you live in a dusty or rural area?
★ Do you have pets (and if so, how many)?
★ Do you suffer from allergies or asthma?
★ Are you naturally tidy?

These variables can affect the level of dirt—and dirt tolerance—in your home. You have to determine what level of cleanliness you want to maintain in your household.

1–2 PEOPLE IN THE HOME
BASIC CLEANING MONTHLY
DEEP CLEANING EVERY OTHER MONTH

2–4 PEOPLE IN THE HOME
BASIC CLEANING EVERY OTHER WEEK
DEEP CLEANING EVERY OTHER MONTH

4–6 PEOPLE IN THE HOME
BASIC CLEANING EVERY WEEK
DEEP CLEANING MONTHLY

Starting Place Here's my rule of thumb, *right,* to help you determine a cleaning schedule that works for a "normal" household with non-allergic family members to maintain an average level of clean.

Health Alert Households with family members who have asthma, allergies, or other respiratory ailments clean more frequently to control the elements that trigger problems.

Make Basic Cleaning the simple process it should be, not an overwhelming chore. These quick tips for tools and techniques save time.

★ A microfiber cleaning cloth can clean 90 percent of the surfaces in your home (glass, mirrors, leather, brass, marble, oak, walls, and laminate) without chemicals. Plus, using a microfiber cloth to clean these surfaces—instead of using several different tools—saves valuable time. These are available at supermarkets and discount stores.

★ A genuine ostrich feather duster works beautifully on pictures, window blinds, wall hangings, and knickknacks. Your bookshelves, computer and television screens, and entertainment centers can be easily dusted in a few seconds without chemicals. Actual ostrich feathers are black; those colorful feather dusters may have plastic spines that can scratch surfaces.

★ A half damp/half dry microfiber cloth dusts windowsills, lamps, baseboards, and electronics in seconds. Keep extra microfiber cloths on hand for quick cleaning on glass-front doors, glass coffee tables, stainless steel refrigerators, and more. You can wipe these clean in just seconds!

★ Use a lightweight cordless vacuum or electric broom to clean up everyday messes. The kids' cookie crumbs, scattered pet food, and everyday dirt can be picked up in a minute or less with a hand-held vacuum or electric broom. You can find these tools at discount stores for as little as $20.

Ready to Speed Clean

Once you have achieved a base level by completing Basic Cleaning, these tips and products will let you Speed Clean your kitchen and bath.

★ Glass cleaner with a disinfectant cleans kitchen counters and bathrooms in just minutes. Take a walk down the grocery store aisle and you'll be surprised at how many new products are on the shelves.

> **TIP** I found a glass cleaner with a disinfectant built in that kills germs and bacteria in 45 seconds—but not all products work that quickly. Read the product labels, as there are still products that require a 10-minute dwell time on the surface to kill all the germs and bacteria to properly disinfect the surface.

★ Use cooking spray on all pots, pans, and casserole dishes. Hard baked-on food is difficult and time-consuming to clean. A quick spritz of cooking spray will save you time in the kitchen.

★ Fill the sink with hot soapy water and let the dishes soak for a few minutes before putting them in the dishwasher to loosen stuck-on food and eliminate scrubbing.

There are also several new scrubbing tools on the market that are both fun and effective. One company offers a battery-operated dish-scrubbing brush. A European manufacturer produces a sponge that can absorb 20 times its weight and has an aggressive scrubby pad that won't scratch your non-stick surfaces, plastic, or other delicate items. These products are available at most grocery stores, hardware stores, and home centers.

★ Place a box of disinfectant wipes next to each sink to keep your sinks, counters, and toilets clean. They take only about 20 seconds to use. Use shower sprays to prevent mold, soap-scum buildup, and hard-water spots.

★ Keep a bucketless flat mop on hand. These include the battery operated ones that have a container of cleaning solution attached to the handle. Mops with disposable wipes or microfiber pads are the answer to keeping your floors looking clean all the time. Quick spills are no longer a chore to clean: just put on the wipe and clean your floor in less than 5 minutes.

★ Start a NO CLUTTER rule. Keep kitchen countertops clear of appliances, toasters, canisters, can openers, and other paraphernalia. Store these items in the kitchen cabinets or drawers. You will find your kitchen immediately looks cleaner, and clutter-free countertops are so much easier to clean.

Deep Cleaning and Seasonal Cleaning

Deep Cleaning involves the more ambitious or detailed tasks that are done monthly or seasonally: cleaning light fixtures by hand, wiping all the baseboards, removing buildup from surfaces, etc. Deep Cleaning means the complete cleaning of a room from ceiling to floor. This is the time to deal with those areas you do not clean during your routine Basic Cleaning.

Deep Cleaning is more time-consuming than Basic Cleaning, so you'll need to allow more time. Basic Cleaning an average home may take one to two hours. Deep Cleaning can take as long as four to 10 hours—depending on how long it has been since your last Deep Cleaning and how many hands you can find to help accomplish the task.

Many people deep clean twice a year—once in spring and once in fall. Some people rigidly adhere to this schedule. This concept comes from times past, when houses were sealed airtight in the wintertime. In spring, we want to get rid of winter's grime and stale air. In autumn, as leaves begin to turn, we want to rid our homes of the dead bugs, cobwebs, and dust of summer before we retreat indoors for winter.

I don't want you to get overwhelmed by this list. Throughout the book I will be giving you many ways to save time and hard work simply by using the proper tools and techniques, such as using cleaning caddies to group supplies for specific tasks. This list may look like a lot, but you can actually do it quite quickly if you are organized and motivated.

Deep Cleaning Tasks

- ★ Clean ceiling fans
- ★ Clean light fixtures
- ★ Dust ceilings for cobwebs
- ★ Clean heating and cooling vents
- ★ Wash walls (as needed)
- ★ Vacuum drapery (or dry clean)
- ★ Mid-dust the entire room (See Glossary, p. 186)
- ★ Dust behind dressers, refrigerators, headboards, and TVs
- ★ Dust (by hand) knickknacks, pictures, artwork, etc.
- ★ Vacuum furniture, removing the cushions to vacuum the interior of the furniture and moving the furniture to vacuum beneath it
- ★ Clean interior windows
- ★ Vacuum and spot-clean carpet or do total carpet cleaning if needed
- ★ Clean miniblinds
- ★ Change air/furnace filters
- ★ Clean the stove, refrigerator, and microwave—inside and out

Seasonal Cleaning Tasks

Do all of the above PLUS

- ★ Clean interior/exterior of the windows as well as the screens
- ★ Wash exterior entrances and driveway
- ★ Wash curtains and draperies
- ★ Clean window treatments, valances, shades, and blinds
- ★ Clean fireplaces
- ★ Clean patio furniture
- ★ Organize closets
- ★ Clean the barbecue grill

Routinely doing these tasks reduces your workload because keeping everything well maintained allows quick cleanups rather than major scrubbing jobs.

House Cleaning Tip

Make the house inviting quickly. People judge your home by the way it looks and smells. Your closet could be piled a mile high with junk and be the most disorganized place in the world, but keep this secret. Your company will form a quick opinion of your home from their eyes, ears, and nose. Does your home look neat and orderly? A strewn newspaper or stack of magazines can make your living room look disordered. What will guests hear? Dogs that continually bark, loud music, or blaring televisions are less than welcoming. Does your home smell good? If your household includes pets or smokers, or you cook foods with strong odors, you may want to purchase an air purifier or use an air neutralizer spray to keep the air smelling fresh.

Spruce-Up Cleaning
(AKA "mother-in-law is on her way")

Spruce-Up Cleaning is simply a light cleaning of surfaces. Spruce-Up Cleaning is used primarily when unexpected company is on the way and you want your house to look great. Or you might Spruce-Up your house before you leave in the morning so you know that your house will look great when you get home, easing the stress of whatever the day might bring.

This cleaning process is easy and can be done in 15 to 20 minutes. Best of all, Spruce-Up Cleaning gives you the confidence of knowing that your home can be whisked clean as quickly and efficiently as a firefighter puts on gear.

Think of Spruce-Up Cleaning as the epitome of Speed Cleaning 101: How to get your house clean, disinfected, looking good, and smelling good as if you'd spent the whole day cleaning, using fewer chemicals, cool cleaning tools, and less work—but in just minutes!

A 30-Minute Spruce-Up:

★ Shine up bathrooms—sinks, mirrors, and toilets (5 minutes)
★ Shine up kitchen appliances, countertops, and sinks (5 minutes)
★ Vacuum the high traffic areas only (10 minutes)
★ Spot-mop floors and entries (5 minutes)
★ Tidy magazines, pillows, and throws (2 minutes)
★ Pick up mail, toys, and newspapers (3 minutes)

Total cleaning time: 30 minutes or less

The Secret—A Good Strategy

1. Analyze the tasks to be done based on what people will see. Where will the company be? At which door will they arrive? In which room of the house will you congregate?

2. Start with the visual cleaning tasks. I like to start at the front door as a guest would do on arrival. I then proceed with a laundry basket through the areas they will see, removing anything that makes the room look disorganized. View your rooms as if you were a nosy neighbor. It will only take a minute to see the clutter that your company will notice right away.

Now You Can Speed Clean Your Way Through the Rest of the Spruce-Up

1. **Straighten magazine, pillows, rugs, etc. (5 minutes)** This is one of the easiest cleaning tasks to do, and yet it is the most common thing we may miss. We tend to focus on the big things and then miss the straightening task. This happens frequently when we are running around hurrying to pick up our home for the unexpected company.

2. **Spot-vacuum only high-traffic areas that need it. (5 minutes)** This is not the time to clean the carpet wall to wall. This is the time to freshen up the carpet fibers and pull the dirt out of the traffic areas that make a room look messy. Stick to vacuuming the room just enough to make it look clean and inviting.

3. Straighten bedrooms. (5 minutes) Use a three-step process: clean floors, make beds, declutter dresser tops. For children's rooms, close the doors and forget about them. Many parents stress needlessly over the condition of children's rooms. Just think with vision—one day they will move out and you can redecorate. Until the day for rehabbing your child's room arrives, focus on:

★ **Clean floors.** Your children may shove everything from toys to games to empty candy wrappers under the bed, but a bed skirt will hide all that. Make keeping the floor clean a rule by enforcing the 10-minute daily pickup.

★ **Make beds.** A bed that is made makes a room look clean and organized, and children easily can do this. A child learns to make the bed pretty fast when you:
A. Threaten bodily harm
B. Throw the TV out the window while she is watching cartoons
C. Remove the game system, controllers, and memory cards from the entertainment area.
For teenagers who are going through their rebellious stage, look for areas of compromise, such as letting them sleep on top of the covers or removing the bed and purchasing an air mattress—tell them it's a new hi-tech bed. Don't you love being a parent?

★ **Declutter dresser tops.** I think a messy dresser top makes the whole room look messy. Limit dresser tops to decorative items. Keep perfumes, loose change, shoehorns, tie clips, jewelry boxes, collectibles, and other items close by in one of the drawers versus collecting dust on the top of your dressers.

4. Clean bathrooms. (5 minutes) The 5-minute bathroom cleaning is one of my favorite tips! A study shows that 44 percent of people responding said cleaning the toilet is the worst household chore. The bathroom has a bad cleaning image. Personally, I think it is actually one of the easiest rooms to clean. The bathroom typically is one of the smallest rooms, and a small room to clean is a plus.

Bathroom-cleaning products are multipurpose and do the work for you. Instead of scrubbing for 20 minutes, you just have to spray, rinse, and shine—if you keep up the cleaning on a regular basis.

5. **Clean floors. (5 minutes)** Use a flat microfiber mop with a mild cleaner for quick mopping. Keep in mind that you do not always need chemicals on your kitchen and hardwood floors. Water removes the soap residue and light dirt that dull floors.

6. **Create ambience. (5 minutes)** Dim the lights in less-than-perfect rooms. Light some scented candles to create a warm and inviting atmosphere. Check for unpleasant odors: Step outside the front door take a few breaths of fresh air, then walk in your home and take a big sniff. If you have cats or dogs and cannot detect any odor, chances are your nose may be a little desensitized, so ask a good friend or family member for an opinion.

7. **Freshen yourself up.** You have just finished the aerobic Speed Cleaning Spruce Up in half the time it would normally take to clean house—and that's a real ego boost. This gives you time to prepare yourself for guests. When answering the door to greet company, look calm and refreshed—even if you are having a stressful day. (Unless, of course, you are trying to play the martyr domestic slave to your mother-in-law, in which case it is good to look like you have been slaving away for hours. Yes, it would be good if Grandma could babysit the children tomorrow so you and your husband can have a date night.)

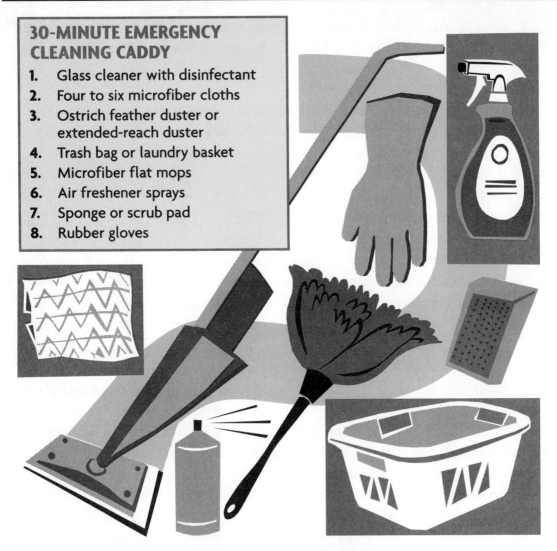

30-MINUTE EMERGENCY CLEANING CADDY

1. Glass cleaner with disinfectant
2. Four to six microfiber cloths
3. Ostrich feather duster or extended-reach duster
4. Trash bag or laundry basket
5. Microfiber flat mops
6. Air freshener sprays
7. Sponge or scrub pad
8. Rubber gloves

Read Product Labels

If there is one thing as a society that we do not do, I would have to say it is reading product labels. When is the last time you flipped over the product and read the back of a bottle of glass cleaner or a box of baking soda? More often than not, we barely read the front label. If it says glass cleaner, soap scum cleaner, or hard water remover, it must be so. Why question the ingredients? Who has the time to read all that mumbo jumbo? Unfortunately, not many of us. Something as simple as using a cleanser that contains bleach with a glass cleaner that contains ammonia can have fatal results.

True Cleaning Confession

One housecleaner did not realize that the cleanser she was using contained bleach. She mixed the cleanser with full-strength ammonia to remove soap scum. The results were dangerous. That chemical combination produces toxic gas. She immediately had trouble breathing and developed a severe headache. She went to the emergency room to discover that she had started to asphyxiate. The toxic gas went directly to her lungs. Fortunately, she got out of the room quickly and did not have any respiratory damage.

When we think about such health mishaps, a question arises. Why don't we read the precautionary statements on product labels? My philosophy is that we're so inundated with words that we tune out labels.

One day during a visit to New York City, I was in Times Square, and the scents, sounds, and sights overwhelmed my senses. I realized the incredible amount of information the brain has to process in a short amount of time. From that experience, I came to realize how desensitized we can become. Each day our brain processes information based on priority levels, so when it comes to mundane tasks like reading the label on a bottle of glass cleaner, we tend to ignore it. After all, it's just glass cleaner, right?

I have learned the hard way how damaging some cleaning products can be to our health and to our home's surfaces. So please read the product labels, and always try to use chemicals and products that have no harsh fumes.

Cosmetic Cleaning

After cleaning many homes and offices, I have become dismayed about the number of worn or damaged surfaces that have been ruined by improper cleaning methods. I have seen hardwood floors that have lost their polyurethane shine and look chalky white. I have seen countless dull no-wax floors. I have seen scratched and nicked kitchen cabinets. And I have seen bathrooms with eroded tile grout and fixtures that no longer have a chrome finish due to acid-based cleaners.

I have made it my mission to teach proper, safe cleaning techniques for all your home surfaces and how to repair problems. I have developed a cleaning method that can save you thousands of dollars. I call it Cosmetic Cleaning.

Cosmetic Cleaning is making an old or damaged surface look like new again. In most cases, it's quite easy, and the results are incredible. So before you think about refinishing your worn wood floor or ripping out bathroom tile with the ugly grout, try these Cosmetic Cleaning techniques.

Quick Cosmetic Cleaning Tips

1. **Clean stove drip pans.** I used to drive myself crazy trying to clean these. I could clean them every time I cooked, or I could let them go and face built-up grime eventually. I tried throwing them in the dishwasher, but although it did clean off most of the grime, the drip pans lost their luster. With Cosmetic Cleaning, you need never fret about cleaning your drip pans. Go to a superstore and buy four brand-new drip pans, but keep the old, dirty drip pans. Put the old ones on the stove when you cook; clean them periodically to avoid grease buildup. Whenever you have company, however, use the new, shiny drip pans.

2. **Rejuvenate dining chairs and table.** If your upholstered seat cushions are stained, throw on slipcovers. For wooden chairs, tie-on seat cushions can do wonders; plus, you can purchase plastic seat covers to protect the cushions. What a great idea when you have young children! It's also easy to rejuvenate wood tables that have water damage or scratches. Treat them with lemon oil at least once a month. For tables that have a damaged polyurethane protective finish, try a product that combines a furniture stain and polyurethane. Check with furniture manufacturers for instructions on re-staining prior to starting, but in most cases, you can lightly sand the wood, or clean the surface with steel wool to prepare for staining. Then, for about $15 you can give your kitchen

table a dramatic new look: Purchase a small bouquet of flowers ($6), new place mats ($8), two scented candles ($1). With just a little creativity you can make your table inviting.

3. **Whiten tile grout.** It doesn't take long for bathroom or kitchen grout to show the effects of hard water and soap scum deposits. It starts to look dingy, dirty, and old. There is an easy remedy. Clean the grout by applying peroxide full strength from a spray bottle. Let it sit on the surface for three to five minutes. You also can use a tile mold and mildew killer. Or you can make your own tile cleaner by mixing 1 part bleach and 4 parts water; let it sit on the surface for 10 minutes, then rinse. Let clean surfaces dry completely. Then apply a little grout white. Grout white is a bit of a misnomer because it comes in many colors that match popular grout tints. It is something like shoe polish; you rub it into your grout. After that, apply grout sealer to prevent future dirt buildup. The sealer comes in a tube that is ready to use and has a tip that fits perfectly into the grout space openings. Look for these products at home centers, hardware stores, and supermarkets. Another useful product is a bleach pen, which looks like a fat marker and sells for about $3. The pointed tip dispenses the bleach in just the thin grout area where whitening is needed. Most supermarkets carry these pens, often in the laundry section.

4. **Clean shower doors.** If your shower doors look white, chalky, and etched, the culprits are soap scum and lime scale deposits from hard water. For tough hard-water spots, buy a lime-scale cleanser that has no harsh fumes from your local home center. It removes hard-water stains in minutes. To keep the white, chalky deposits from building up, try wiping down the door with lemon oil twice a month. You also can get a small rubber squeegee (made for use in showers) and squeegee the water off the shower walls and door each time the shower is used. If you don't see improvement from these methods, it may be because shower doors are older and the glass is permanently damaged. You still have a few choices. The easiest is to disguise the ugly shower doors. Install a rod and put up a decorative shower curtain. Hanging the curtain on the outside of the shower door keeps it from getting dirty while it hides the damaged glass panels. Finally, you can replace the doors.

5. Remove carpet stains. First, try a professional carpet spot-cleaner. The best products come from janitorial supply companies (most sell to the public). It's nice to use professional products. You can find specific carpet spot-cleaners for red stains (as from powdered drink mixes), coffee, ink, rust, and more.

No time to tackle those old permanent carpet stains? For a short-term solution to carpet stains, throw down some new carpet runners and rugs. It will give your room a quick face-lift and add a little flair. For a longer-term solution, you can have your carpet professionally dyed at a fraction of the cost of purchasing new carpeting. Look in the phone book to find a local carpet-dyeing company. Most carpet companies use a "cookie cutter" for permanent stains—they cut out the damaged spot and replace it with clean carpet from a closet or other inconspicuous place.

6. Touch up scratched and nicked oak doors and woodwork. Wood-stain pens are available in a variety of colors. You can cover most scratches in minutes. For cabinets that need a face-lift, use a polyurethane stain. In just a few hours your cabinets can look new and shiny for less than $20.

7. **Repair tears on leather furniture or vinyl.** Items can be repaired in minutes with leather-repair kits. I was amazed by the results. For more information, sign on to the Internet and search for a liquid-leather product.

8. **Restore dull and worn hardwood floors.** Give them a face-lift with a hardwood floor restorer. With this product, you safely mop on a new finish that restores the shine. Or, you also can rejuvenate hardwood by cleaning your floor (a neutral cleaner is always your best bet for hardwood floors) and letting it dry. Then apply a fresh coat of polyurethane. Visit your local hardware store or home center for the necessary tools and products.

9. **Freshen frazzled and worn bed comforters.** Try a new duvet and throw pillows to make your bedding look spiffy and new! You can find complete bedding sets in beautiful colors and prints at most department stores and clearance centers. A new comforter, some throw pillows, and yard sale vases or accessories can make your bedroom a place of peace and tranquility.

10. **Rejuvenate worn and dull laminate countertops.** There is a laminate repair kit you can use easily. These repair kits are available online, in most hardware stores, and at home centers. You also can call in a professional to have your laminate countertops re-sprayed. Check your local telephone listings for this service. For more information on resurfacing cabinets, countertops, and appliances, check out *www.surfacedoctor.com*.

11. **Fix dishwasher racks that have exposed metal that is corroded and gets rust on your dishes.** There are dishwasher-rack repair kits available that come in a variety of colors. These include rubber tips that fit on spokes and enamel paints that cover rust spots on racks.

12. **Keep glasses from coming out of the dishwasher looking chalky and etched.** Do you find that your glassware never looks clean? If so, try a dishwasher detergent with a rinsing agent that helps prevent water spots and protects glassware from etching, such as ShineShield™.

Preventive Cleaning

Preventive Cleaning involves finding creative ways to stop the dirt and buildup before it starts. For example, it's preventive cleaning when you use floor mats to stop the dirt from even starting in your home. Here are some Preventive Cleaning tips to help keep the dirt from starting in your home.

Quick Preventive Cleaning Tips

★ **Keep bathroom exhaust fans running** the entire time you are taking a bath or shower and for 30 minutes afterward. This lowers the humidity that supports mold growth in bathroom grout and shower tracks.

★ **Don't use a bath soap that leaves a chalky white residue** on the bathtub walls and shower doors. My husband used to shower with a deodorant soap that did this. Once we switched soaps, the bathroom tile become much easier to clean.

★ **Use the lemon-oil-on-your-shower-doors tip** I recommend applying it to the shower doors twice a month. Two to three teaspoons of lemon oil on a dry cloth should leave a thin layer of lemon oil. Apply in overlapping horizontal strokes, not in a circular pattern. The oil makes shampoo, soap scum, and grimy water bead up on the glass, then roll down the drain.

★ **Keep windows and garage doors closed** to keep dust from getting into your home. Leaving doors and windows open just makes more dusting work for you! If you like to keep your windows open, use window filters that keep airborne particulates and dust out of your home (available at *www.nationalallergysupply.com).* Then you can still enjoy a fresh breeze on a beautiful day.

★ **Use a mold killer** that will last two years, preventing further growth in the shower or bathtub area. (This is available at *www.nationalallergysupply.com).* If you have had problems with mold, it makes perfect sense to purchase a mold inhibitor.

★ **Purchase an after-shower spray and use it after every shower.** Do not rinse the cleaner off the surface. I confess my husband is consistent. (So why should I spray when he does such a great job?) Our home is three years old and has poor bathroom ventilation, but we have never have had mold growth or soap scum buildup. I wish I could tell you it's because we are so clean, but alas, that would not be true! The shower sprays work incredibly well. There even is a product that attaches to the showerhead. After taking your shower, push a button and the cleaner sprays the shower stall. It's practically a self-cleaning shower! This tip will make your shower cleanup easy and stress-free. You can find after-shower sprays at the grocery store.

★ **Avoid mold and mildew** If you live in a region where the humidity is high and mold and mildew grow easily, you can prevent growth the next time you paint your home. You can use paint that contains mildewcides, or mix in a mold and mildew preventive additive. Think of all the places that you won't have to clean mold again—basement and exterior walls, decks, railings—anywhere that mold likes to grow. It works great with all interior latex, oil-, and solvent-based paints as well as stains and coatings.

★ **Place a toilet-cleaning tablet in the tank** It will keep the toilet cleaner in between scrubbing. This helps prevent the lime-scale ring you get in toilets that are used rarely. Some bathroom cleaners actually help keep your toilet bowl cleaner longer. They cling to the toilet bowl and will not dissipate like normal cleaners. Homeowners should never let their pets drink out of the toilet. If your pet does sneak in and drink from the stool, never leave any type of cleaner in your toilet bowl unattended.

★ **Use grout sealer** (available at home centers) to treat the grout on ceramic tile, terrazzo, marble, and granite floors. Whenever you purchase a new hard floor, it is important that the grout is sealed, an inexpensive and easy job. You can buy the sealer at a home center and mop it or brush it into the grout, following the directions on the product label. Let the sealer dry the recommended amount of time for maximum benefit. Most contractors who install new floors fail to mention that sealing your grout will extend the beauty and life of your floors. Sealing the grout also will protect it from harsh chemicals, erosion, and stains. Sealed grout is easier to clean and lasts longer.

★ **Clean the refrigerator** Place shelf liners in the refrigerator drawers. They sell these at your grocery store. Liners prevent you from having to take the drawer out to clean; just replace the liners when dirty and wipe drawer sides and fronts clean. For dried-on spills, a handheld steam cleaner works wonders.

★ **Apply a floor restorer or polymer shine on your floors** to preserve their beauty (and to make cleaning them much easier). This works well if you prefer a low luster, matte shine. For older linoleum, or worn-out no-wax floors, try a high-gloss advanced polymer product that protects your floor's finish, especially in high-traffic areas, and seals the floor against dirt and stains. Preventing dirt from imbedding in the textured indentations of your floor greatly reduces your cleaning time. When shopping for a no-wax or vinyl floor, run your finger across the sample surface. If it feels bumpy and rough with the pattern, stay away from that type of floor. Many days I have had to scrub no-wax floors with a grout brush and toothbrush to remove embedded dirt from the indentations. Ideally, choose a floor that has a smooth surface.

★ **Store trash bags** Store extra liners on the bottom of the trash can. This protects the bottom of the trash can from spills and leaks. If a bag gets soiled you can discard it; otherwise, pull up the next bag as your new liner. Never have a dirty and stinky trash can bottom again!

★ **Clean the microwave.** If you hate to clean the hardened food particles from your microwave, just line the bottom with 10 to 15 paper towels. As they get dirty, immediately throw them in the trash and replace with fresh ones. You will save so much time!

★ **Get spot-free stainless-steel sink fixtures.** Treat with mineral oil to prevent lime-scale buildup and spotting.

★ **Use the dishwasher less.** If you hate to wash dishes all the time, try paper plates for those lazy nights. That will prevent dirty dishes. My 14-year-old son is the primary dishwasher in our home. He is always asking us to use paper plates and limit our drinking-glass usage. Ha! Fat chance of that! He certainly dirtied up plates and glasses when he wasn't on dish duty. It's fun being a parent!

CHAPTER TWO

Getting in the Mood to Clean

One of the biggest problems with housework is how easily you can find ways to procrastinate. Let's face it: We're all a little lazy when it comes to housework. I can think of a hundred things that I'd rather do than housework, can't you?

Cleaning is labor-intensive, and it can be icky and dirty. What can we do to get motivated? What makes us get excited about cleaning? Sometimes it's music, or new cleaning tools, or just a rainy day that motivates us. But the biggest motivator usually is that someone is coming to visit! Yes, this is the reason most of us get started on those overdue cleaning chores. We want everyone to see our home at its best. After all, our home is our castle, and we want to be proud of where we live.

So if no one is about to come for a visit, what can we do to get in the cleaning mood? Everyone has different motivators, but here are a few ideas to get in the mood to clean—and to make the most of your time.

★ **Pick a one- to two-hour time slot for cleaning.** The main thing is to pick the time of day when you feel energetic and can concentrate on the job. Early morning—and I mean early—usually works best for me, because the older I get, the less energy I have by the end of the day. Sometimes I am comatose by 10 p.m., and I pray the house doesn't burn down if the two youngest boys get into mischief! I do my best work when everyone else in the house is sleeping. It can be hard to clean when the kids are getting cereal out of the pantry and your spouse insists that he absolutely must walk across the wet floor.

★ **Think of cleaning as a great way to stay in shape.** Cleaning burns calories, *below,* and you get a clean home at the same time.

In 30 minutes, a 145- to 150-pound person can burn
73 calories doing laundry
68 calories making beds
78 calories washing dishes
85 calories dusting
112 calories sweeping
119 calories vacuuming
102 washing windows

For additional information, go to a free online service at *www.caloriesperhour.com*

★ **Turn on music that makes you feel good.** Just for fun, ask some of your friends and coworkers the type of music they like to listen to while cleaning. You may be surprised at their answers. Some of my friends surprised me with their choices—country, classical, gospel, soul, and more. One of my most conservative friends plays some pretty intense rock 'n' roll when she cleans. Let's face it: It's fun to enhance your cleaning experience and dance while cleaning. Why not let loose and enjoy yourself in the privacy of your own home? Find a radio station or CD that you like and put on headphones.

★ **Put on your cleaning clothes—whatever they may be.** My cleaning clothes are so comfortable, I normally would not wear them outside, even on a short run to the grocery store. Just wearing my cleaning duds keeps me focused on the job. Don't wear favorite clothes. No matter how careful you are, something always spills, or you'll rub against a cleaning product that can discolor fabric. If you need to wear something nice while cleaning, don an apron with pockets. You'll protect your clothes and can fill the pockets with cleaning supplies. I store toothbrushes, grout brushes, an ostrich duster, and other useful items in the pockets.

★ **Reread your favorite chapter of a "how to be a go-getter" book.**
Then get up and go to work.

★ **Try a little coffee, tea, or a soft drink to perk you up.** If it's the
physical energy you lack, and you don't want to try the caffeine
route, there are so many healthy natural energy boosters, like
ginseng, or energy booster drinks. My personal favorite is an
energy drink. But please don't write to tell me it's bad for me;
I like the extra boost it gives me! And believe it or not, a benefit
of cleaning is that it gets you moving, lowers your stress, and
boosts your energy.

★ **Turn off the phone or let the answering machine take your calls.**
Have you ever felt like your cell phone, cordless phone, or pager
is nothing more than an electronic leash around your neck? These
items give people easy access to call you any time, any place.

I have felt my electronic leash pull at me many times. It normally happens when my hands are full with groceries or greasy from forming hamburger mixture into balls before cooking. Don't get me wrong; I am not anti-technology. It's just when you're trying to clean, your hands are wet, you're bending over the shower scrubbing, and suddenly *brrrringgg, brrringggg* ... arghhhh! You lose five minutes of cleaning time—and a ton of motivation—just by answering the phone. However, if you are a chatty person who can multitask, and you actually like talking to someone on the phone while you clean, then keep on talking!

★ **Turn off the television if it distracts you.** If you cannot trust yourself to stay focused around a television and you think it will slow you down while cleaning your home, just turn it off! Many times my children start out with the best intentions of cleaning their rooms or doing a chore. As the TV drones in the background, somehow a cartoon, game show, or movie draws them back to the set, where they sit hypnotized and forget the chore they are supposed to be doing. The same thing happens with adults; the TV can be a distraction. The minute we sit down to watch it, we lose our momentum and motivation.

★ **Ask everyone who is not working to get out of the house or out of the way.** Anyone in your family can be bitten by the cleaning bug—you, your spouse, or the kids (you'd be surprised). When the cleaning bug bites a family member, just get out of the way! For example, my husband gets bitten by the cleaning bug about twice a year. He grabs his boom box, turns on some great tunes, and that man is motivated to clean. Give him a new power-cleaning tool, hand-held steamer, pressure washer, or window-cleaning system on a telescopic pole, and he is in hog heaven. When he starts to clean the garage, everyone in the house scatters. It's not that we're being lazy or don't want to help him; it's just that he will ask questions that have no answers. He may mutter questions under his breath, ask them aloud to himself, ask a passer-by, or direct them to the universe. Most husbands ask these same questions: "How did this place become such a wreck? Where did all this stickiness come from? Can't the kids get some of these shoes out of here? How many pairs of skates do the children need? Why are we keeping tennis rackets when no one has played in three years? Why are the mice using our patio furniture cushion as a multifamily dwelling?" Enough said! Just take advantage of the extra help—man, woman or child—and let the cleaning bug take over your family!

★ **Hire a sitter for small children, or clean while they sleep.** Children younger than 5 tend to have short attention spans and require more of your time. Attempting to speed clean your home with little people following you around can hinder your system. Take advantage of play groups, preschool times, and nap times to get your home in order.

★ **Children age 5 years and older can be fantastic helpers.** For the Fourth of July weekend, my 5-year-old cousin Jessica from Dallas came to visit with her family. She would get up early every morning with me and watch me bang pots and pans as I hustled up breakfast for 11 people. Jessica, wearing her little pink Cinderella pajamas, jumped right into the kitchen chaos, cleaning and cooking. She helped me make quiche, Bananas Foster, and French toast. She helped load the dishwasher, clear the table, and sweep the floor. Then she mopped the floor. Jessica did something families have been doing for years: She developed a relationship with me just by sharing everyday household chores. Cleaning and cooking together created a special memory for both of us.

Organize Your Cleaning Supplies

★ **Gather your cleaning supplies before you start.** If you are ready to clean, all the supplies and equipment must also be ready to go. Purchase multipurpose products, washable cleaning cloths, and cleaning tools that store nicely in a caddy or basket. Doing this helps you move through out your home quickly and more efficiently than you may have been in the past.

★ **Make a chore list for each family member.** This is one thing I've done with my five children. I post the list on the refrigerator and hold each child accountable for his or her tasks. The chores are age-appropriate, and the children learn the value of teamwork and doing their fair share. A chore list can be organized with each child's name and his/her chores for that particular day or week.

★ **Have enough supplies for your helpers.** If you are incorporating family members into your routine, plan for each person to have a basket or pail to carry supplies. What you put in the cleaning caddy depends on the job. It is very frustrating for a person doing a job to continually have to borrow glass cleaner, cleanser, or dusters from someone else to get the job done. Stock caddies at the beginning of the task, just like the supervisors who stock the hotel maids' carts.

★ **Buy cleaning tools that will do a lot of the work for you.** One walk down the grocery store aisle should convince you that cleaning does not have to be done the old-fashioned way any longer. There are toilet brushes with flushable cleaning tips, mops with disposable pads, disinfectant wipes for quick touch-ups—myriad items that will get the job done quickly. If you are still scrubbing and rubbing until your shoulders are sore, this book will change all that!

The Mental Game of Cleaning

★ **Focus on the after-cleaning feeling.** It does feel good when it's done! When you're overwhelmed with a cleaning task, focus on the end result: Create a mental picture of a clean, great-smelling home, and see yourself taking a moment to enjoy it.

★ **Think of cleaning as therapeutic and meditative.** These activities don't require a great deal of brain power, so they give you time to decompress and think about other things. Some artists and inventors say that their greatest ideas come to them while they are doing repetitive, low-thought tasks, such as cleaning, showering, etc. Who knows what great things might come to you while you clean? Many people who work part-time in the janitorial company in the evenings have full-time day jobs as teachers or other professionals. When asked on the application why they want to work a janitorial position, the most common answer is because the job does not require brain power. One man shared that it helped him decompress after a hard day of office duties. Women have told me they find housecleaning chores to be calming—once they find the time to do them.

★ **Compete against yourself.** Time yourself and see if you can get faster every time you perform a task. An average Speed Cleaner should be able to clean approximately 1,000 square feet an hour. This industry rate in residential home cleaning has been standardized for years. It may sound difficult at first, but it is an achievable goal—especially after reading this book. This is what the speedy maid services aim for in cleaning your home. The nicest thing about speed cleaning is that you are not cleaning harder, sweating through room-to-room cleaning. You're using the techniques, tools, and timesaving tips that enable you to do the work faster and easier. You'll be doing less work in less time. What a great deal for just the cost of this book!

Time for Professional Help

If you just can't get motivated to clean no matter how hard you try, it's time to hire a maid service! Why? The answer is not what you think it is. Rather than letting you off the hook, hiring a professional often forces people to clean before the cleaning service comes! (We all know it's OK if we see our dirt, but we don't like it when someone else does!) I have traveled across the country many times to speak at home and garden shows. It never fails: During the course of the weekend a man will come up to me and say, "I love to clean. But my wife (or girlfriend) doesn't. Do you have any tips to get her motivated?" For these men, the solution I give never changes. I instruct each man to buy a gift certificate for a housecleaning service for her next birthday, anniversary, or holiday. She will be elated and give him the biggest "thank you" ever! She will tell her friends how great her man is! He will become the hero in her life. Everything will be smooth sailing until a week before the cleaning crew is scheduled to arrive. At that point, she knows people are going to come into her home and see (and possibly judge) her private domain. That thought kicks the domestic-image reaction into high gear! These women organize closets, clear junk out of the way, tidy clutter that's been around for years—just so the cleaning service can do its job! Have you ever heard friends, neighbors, or coworkers joke about how they clean before the cleaning lady comes? It's true! Guys, give it a try!

Summing It Up–The Last Call for Help

Now that you've found one or two motivational tips that will work for you, I bet you're in the mood to clean through your home like a tornado. But I also know that there are a few of you who hate to clean. For those in the latter group, I have a few more ideas that will help minimize your cleaning work.

Try these ideas to keep your home more clean and organized and to keep your cleaning time to a minimum

1. **Everything in your home needs a place to belong.** It could be a magazine or newspaper basket, a coat rack, or a shoe shelf. If you provide a container, shelf, drawer, or rack for it, the result is less clutter.

2. **Don't put it down, put it away!** An advice columnist once offered this great advice to a lady who wrote to her about being stressed over the clutter in her home. This advice is simple and effective. Make those seven words your daily rule, and learn to be a Speed Cleaning expert and a clean-as-you-go person. Those seven words resonated with me in my quest for the best cleaning methods. I keep those words close to my heart and have repeated them to myself through the years. I've said them to my children as they walked in from school and tried to drop their backpacks on the floor. I believe they will use the same seven words some day with their children.

3. **Choose one room a day to dust and vacuum.** This can be done in five minutes if you never let the room get out of control. This one tip will keep you from having to spend hours at a time cleaning, and it should limit your cleaning sessions to just 15 to 20 minutes. (You already probably spend that much time procrastinating. Just think: You could already be finished!) If you rotate through the rooms of your home, cleaning one a day, you should be able to keep your house clean without ever breaking into a sweat! (If you are the type of person who wants to clean only one time a week or twice a month, that is OK too.)

4. **Shine your bathrooms in just five minutes a day.** This is possible when you use a glass cleaner formulated with a disinfectant or disinfectant wet wipes.

5. Sweep and mop the floors in the high traffic areas as needed. If you are still using one of the old-fashioned string or bacteria-infested sponge mops, switch to a flat mop with a disposable microfiber pad to clean your floor in just five minutes!

CHAPTER THREE

Speed Cleaning Techniques of the Pros

If at times you think cleaning your house is an overwhelming task, imagine cleaning a 10-story building with only five helpers—every day! How would you get through all the dusting, trash pickup, vacuuming, and the mess left by 700 employees, five days a week? In the janitorial industry, professional cleaners are expected to clean 4,000 square feet of commercial space, or 1,000 square feet of residential space, per hour. How big is your home? Can you imagine how much you would be able to accomplish if you could clean at the professional rate? You'd start to feel like a superhero!

Remember that many of my Speed Cleaning tips are based on the training techniques I use to develop programs for chemical manufacturers and my own cleaning-company employees. These techniques have been tested and proven to save time. So what's the secret? How do you get your home clean in half the time just like professionals do?

One reason professional cleaners can clean so quickly is *technique.* A simple change of habit can make a huge difference. For instance, do you clean your dining room table, bathroom mirrors, and microwave in a circular motion or a horizontal overlapping motion? How many times have you cleaned a glass patio door only to see the streaky smears in the late afternoon sunshine? For quick cleaning, a horizontal overlapping stroke takes 50 percent less time, and you will cover the surface evenly—including the corners and sides that are missed by a circular motion.

1) Be organized and have all your supplies on or near you.

2) Clean from top to bottom.

3) Work the room in a circle. Finish one room at a time—no backtracking!

4) Don't clean what's already clean.

Four Basic Principles

So how can you learn the fastest techniques for cleaning your home? You have already learned the Three Ts—Time, Tools, and Techniques. The rest comes from following four basic principles used in the janitorial industry. (After you understand how the principles work, I'll show you how to use the whole process in each room.) The Four Basic Principles address the actual system you will use to clean everything:

1. Be organized and have all your supplies on or near you. A cleaning caddy, a five-gallon pail, a cleaning apron, and a laundry basket are all great places to store your cleaning supplies. Whatever your preference, choose a container big enough to hold all of your supplies to prevent backtracking. Just like a carpenter who has his toolbox or toolbelt always with him and ready, you need the necessary tools and equipment that enable you to do your job.

As mentioned earlier, it's important for hotel maids to have their tools and equipment ready to go. The maids cannot waste time taking an elevator from the 16th floor back to the supply room in the basement to get more products or tools. In the same way, forgetting supplies or equipment and making a special trip to get them can make cleaning your home seem like twice the work. Each time you have to stop to get a missing tool or product, you've added 2 to 3 minutes to your total cleaning time. Multiply that by the number of times it happens and see how quickly you've spent a lot of unproductive time! No wonder you feel as though you can never get the cleaning done.

Clearly, you can see the benefits of organizing before you start. This will save you time and energy. Make a list of the cleaning tasks you are going to do and check them off as you go. As you check them off your list, you are rewarding yourself for yet another task done! Load your cleaning caddy with the supplies you need to get the job done, and get to it.

2. **Clean from top to bottom.** This rule applies to every single thing that you clean in your home. It does not matter whether you are doing Deep Cleaning, Basic Cleaning, or Spruce-Up Cleaning. Tackle every cleaning job from the top to the bottom. This works for cleaning the outside of the refrigerator, wiping the kitchen cabinets, or washing the walls. You will always start at the top and work your way down in horizontal (not circular or vertical) motions.

Why start at the top? The law of gravity is pretty simple: Dust and dirt fall to the floor as you clean. Many people ask me if you should vacuum first—and my answer is always no. You should always dust first, vacuum last. Vacuuming last captures dust and dirt, unless you have a vacuum that blows dust back into the air. We will talk further about vacuum cleaners in chapter five.

Cleaning top to bottom also forces you to look at your ceilings, top of the walls, door and window frames, and high corners. These areas are often overlooked because we tend to pay attention to things at eye level when we clean. Cleaning from top to bottom forces us to check out the entire room and do a more thorough job.

Of course, the other reason we clean from top to bottom is equally important—we are cleaning in a synchronized, organized way, which saves time!

3. Work the room in a circle and finish one room at a time In the janitorial industry every single step is important. If employees do not work an entire office in a circle, they could miss trash, cobwebs, and spots on the walls and furniture. Remembering where you cleaned last is tough if you don't follow an organized approach. This is also true in a home. The phone rings, you let the dog out—and you forget where you stopped cleaning. Working the room in a circle reduces the chance of forgetting where you've cleaned or missing an area. By cleaning each area thoroughly as you work your way around the room, you are less likely to miss anything. And if you have your supply caddy with you at all times, you will avoid backtracking and missing spots.

4. Don't clean what's already clean People often overclean certain areas. For example, how many of you clean the entire glass patio door when there is one dirty spot by the handle or one child's handprints on the glass? You think, "How much more time can it really take to clean the whole thing—a few minutes?" But remember, a few minutes for this, a few minutes for that, the time adds up. Clean the dirty spot and move on to the next task. You can shave hours off your cleaning time by cleaning the dirty areas only and shining up the rest with a slightly damp cloth. The "don't clean what's already clean" concept comes from the "clean smarter, not harder" approach.

Another example: If you have one bathroom shower in your house that gets used rarely, it may only have a little bit of dust in it. Why apply four different cleaners and scrub it as if it needs disinfecting? All you need to do is spray some disinfectant glass cleaner and buff the chrome with a dry cloth. The shower will look shiny and clean in just two minutes!

The best way to learn how not to clean what's already clean is simple: Analyze the cleaning job. Ask yourself: "How dirty is this, and where is it dirty? Does it need a deep cleaning or just a light touch-up?" If it isn't dirty, dust it, shine it, and move on.

True Cleaning Confessions

One exasperated mother of three said she just could not get her house clean without the job taking an entire day. When I started quizzing her about the way in which she cleaned her home, her problem became obvious.

She went up and down the stairs six to eight times, jumped from room to room with no organized approach, and never finished one room before moving on to the next. She just had portions of the home clean. This busy mom had the motivation to clean, but she did not know the proper technique to do so quickly and easily.

Clean Smarter, Not Harder Tips

1. Carry tools that will save you time and energy

★ Use a whisk broom to save time when vacuuming along the edges of carpets and baseboards. A plastic whisk broom works best; you can find them at your local grocery store or discount store. I also use a whisk broom on the steps, between stair railings, on doorjambs, wall vents, and pleated lampshades. A whisk broom also works great for removing the debris underneath your couch cushions.

★ Have a couple of damp cloths over your shoulder to save you the time you would spend running to the sink to saturate the cloths. Damp cloths can be used to clean 90 percent of the surfaces in your home. Typically only 10 percent of the surfaces in your home needs disinfectant cleaners. Brass, marble, leather, solid-surface countertops, fine furniture, and wood surfaces can be dusted with a slightly damp cloth. When cleaning with a damp cloth, I prefer to use the microfiber type. They work well on all surfaces without leaving streaky smears behind.

> **TIP** We overspray, overbuy, and overuse cleaning products on our home surfaces. Many times this causes buildup, gummy fingerprints, and smearing—and more cleanup time! Look for a cleaning product that has a disinfectant already built in. This product will help you reduce cleaning time because you only need to spray the surface with one product.

★ Hang supplies from your belt or vacuum, or put them in your pockets to save time by keeping everything you need at your fingertips. This tip may sound odd to you, but it is one of the best in this book! Think about the carpenter's belt. He keeps his hammer, nails, and other tools right on his body when working. Just think if he had to go up and down a ladder every few minutes for nails while framing a home. Good grief, it would take him twice the time to do his job! Use an apron to hold toothbrushes, grout brushes, cleaning cloths, glass-cleaner bottles, and more. A professional cleaning apron has deep pockets to hold all of those items as well as loops on each side of your hip to hold the bottles. I love my Speed Cleaning apron. If you wear an apron with the bottle "holsters," you may look like a gunslinger ready to draw your guns. The concept really works!

★ Keep glass cleaner near you all the time because you can use it to clean so many things.

★ Use extension dusters to save a lot of time when cleaning ceiling fans and high cobwebs. Forget going to get the ladder, setting it up, climbing up it to clean, and then putting it away! What a waste of time that is!

2. **Let the tools and chemicals do the work**

★ Read product labels and leave the product on the surface as directed to get the best results. (See page 34 for more info on product labels.) You would be surprised how many people rush this step and don't get as much cleaning benefit from a product as they could.

★ Buy scrub brushes on a pole from a janitorial supplier. No more bending in tubs and showers. They will reach far, so you don't have to!

★ Stay away from old-fashioned "home remedy" cleaning solutions that take forever to work.

★ Buy one product that can clean several different things. Read the label and look for a product that cleans rust, lime scale, and soap scum. That just eliminated two extra bottles from your cleaning kit.

3. **Analyze the job and do two things at once**

★ While a chemical is working on the bathroom tile, shine the glass mirror.

★ While you are vacuuming, use a microfiber cloth and duster to dust and vacuum simultaneously.

★ Clean the microwave by zapping a cup of hot water until it boils inside the microwave oven—the steam will work on any spills inside—then wipe the microwave clean with a cloth. Adding lemon juice to the water leaves a fresh scent, and the lemony steam helps cut grease. While that's working, spot-clean the kitchen cabinets.

★ Carry two cloths; use one for dusting and the other to clean glass.

★ Hang one big trash bag on your belt or cleaning caddy to collect household trash instead of running back and forth to empty each wastebasket into the garbage.

Pro Cleaning Methods

In the janitorial industry we have different methods of cleaning: Team Cleaning, Wave Cleaning, and Zone Cleaning. All these methods work well with two people or more.

Team Cleaning

This involves one person being responsible for one specific job task at a time and completing only that job. When Team Cleaning you typically divide the team into four cleaning specialists.

★ **The Bathroom/Kitchen Specialist** Specializes in bathrooms, kitchens, and floors—mainly the wet work. (More on wet work in chapter eight.)

★ **The Vacuum Specialist** Vacuums. Period.

★ **The Utility Specialist** Removes trash, sweeps the floors, and deals with any special tasks.

★ **The Dusting Specialist** Responsible for high-dusting, mid-dusting, and low-dusting. This job typically also includes glass cleaning.

For big families sharing the cleaning tasks, Team Cleaning is a winner. The workers are not as overwhelmed as when cleaning alone, and they tend to do one thing and do it very well. The team approach works even if you only have two people; the trick is in how you divide the work. For example, one person does all the dry work in a room; the other person does all the wet work.

Wave Cleaning

This creative cleaning method is a variation of the Team Cleaning method. You need a team of two to six people. This is a particularly popular method for families that work well as a team.

Think of being in the stands at a ball game and everyone does the wave. In this variation, each person represents a wave of cleaning. The process starts at one end of the house. One example of the division of labor involves four team members: The high duster goes through the room first, then moves on to the next room. Next up, the trash pickup and wall-washing team member comes through. Team member three, the floor washer and bathroom cleaner takes up the action. And finally, the vacuuming and tidying player finishes the room and shuts off the lights.

This process makes the work go quickly, and each person can inspect the other person's work. You can adapt cleaning duties to the needs of the job and the capabilities of the family members. For example, you could have a laundry person, a bathroom person, a vacuum and dusting person, and a floor-washing person. Whatever works best in your home is fine.

Zone Cleaning

This is the term used for someone cleaning one area or zone. Zone Cleaning generally refers to cleaning one room at a time in its entirety.

CHAPTER FOUR

Your Pro
Cleaning Kit

How many cleaning products do you have in your housecleaning arsenal right now? If you are like most people, I would guess anywhere from 10 to 20 products, including glass cleaners, furniture cleaners, toilet cleaners, rust cleaners, shower cleaners. Many people believe that more is better when it comes to cleaning products. We tend to overbuy, overspend, overspray, and overwork with them. However, most homes can be cleaned using only four or five main products. Hoarding cleaning supplies is like keeping those old clothes we are sure we will fit into again someday—we don't need them.

I have come a long way as a professional Speed Cleaner, and now I have streamlined my cleaning kit to four basic cleaners. I also have a specialist cleaning kit for the cleaning projects that need to be tackled only once a month or so. I can't tell you the amount of time and money this has saved me. Another reason to downsize your cleaning chemicals? Storing too many cleaning products can affect your health and that of your family. Here is a new twist for you. The Environmental Protection Agency (EPA) states that indoor air can be two to three times more contaminated than outdoor air. How can that be? Isn't the air inside cleaner than the air outside? No, for a variety of reasons.

True Cleaning Confessions

Many years ago I was a cleaning product junkie. I had so many stacked underneath my kitchen sink and stocked in my cleaning caddy that they would fall to the floor every time I tried to clean. I didn't (and couldn't) feel organized. Stopping every time something fell out of my cleaning caddy, picking it up, and wrestling it back into the overloaded caddy was annoying and time-wasting. It was also frustrating to see so many different products at the grocery store and not know which ones really worked. The packaging looked good, and the promises on the labels sounded great, but many of the products did not do what they claimed. Purchasing many of these products was a total waste of my money, but I felt as though I should keep them.

Indoor Air Contaminants

Airborne allergens are invisible to the naked eye. They float around your home in ordinary house dust, enter your nasal passages, are inhaled through your mouth, and are ingested into your system.

Harsh and toxic products (such as bleach and ammonia) that are stored in plastic bottles can emit chemical gases into our homes' air. These gases can then mix with other fumes, causing pollution that can make us sick. The plastic bottle may never leak, but fumes can seep out through the container. These fumes are commonly referred to as Volatile Organic Compounds (VOCs) that contaminate indoor air.

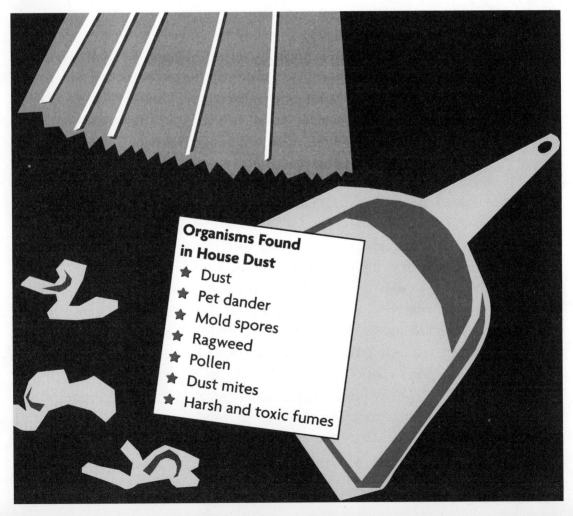

Organisms Found in House Dust
- ★ Dust
- ★ Pet dander
- ★ Mold spores
- ★ Ragweed
- ★ Pollen
- ★ Dust mites
- ★ Harsh and toxic fumes

True Cleaning Confessions

I've heard of people getting sick every time they enter their home. They suffer headaches, nausea, and other symptoms. When they go away for the weekend or on vacation, their symptoms clear up. One person found, after many doctor visits, that the culprit was a bottle of household bleach stored under the kitchen sink. Feeling better was as simple as moving the bleach out of the living area. Most of us would never even think that the cleaning caddy is a source of toxic air pollution. But the truth is certain cleaning products, such as liquid bleach and ammonia, should never be mixed or stored together. It's like storing combustible materials next to a can of lighter fluid or gasoline. Bad idea.

TIP Store ordinary household bleach in a well-ventilated area, such as in the garage, so if it releases fumes it won't pollute your household air.

Improve Your Home's Indoor Air Quality

It is easier than you think to improve the indoor air of your home. Prevent the things that cause poor indoor air.

- ★ Keep indoor humidity below 50 percent. You can buy hygrometers (humidity meters) at hardware stores.
- ★ Run exhaust fans while showering and for 30 minutes afterward to reduce humidity that encourages mildew.
- ★ Consider purchasing a hood vent for the stove in a kitchen without vents or windows.
- ★ Vent the clothes dryer outside or through the attic.
- ★ Invest in an attic fan. These help whole-house ventilation by efficiently circulating indoor air and reduce cooling costs by venting hot air.

★ Pull up carpet on a damp basement floor if mold growth starts, kill mold, and use a dehumidifier to deter regrowth.

★ Control dust mites by encasing pillows and mattresses with allergen-protective covers. Wash bedding weekly in 130 degree or hotter water.

★ Keep closets cool and dry, and do not store wet clothing, which could mildew.

★ Reduce pet dander allergies by bathing dogs and cats with allergen shampoo.

★ Repair all leaks and water damage (such as around windows, from the roof, or in the basement). It only takes 24 hours for mold to grow.

★ Keep windows and doors closed during allergy season to keep out pollen and ragweed spores.

★ Houseclean on a regular basis. It can make all the difference.

★ Choose cleaning products that emit no harsh fumes.

★ Clean vents. Dirty heating and air-conditioning systems kick up allergens.

★ Change filters on humidifiers and dehumidifiers.

★ Check refrigerator drip pans monthly; wipe clean.

★ Vacuum pet hair from carpets and furnishings daily.

★ Dust regularly, using cloths that capture the dust; wash cloths after each use.

★ Purchase a HEPA filter vacuum. It will capture 97 percent of airborne particulate matter down to 0.3 micron in size. (For more on vacuum filters, see chapter six.)

Your Pro Cleaning Kit

An automobile mechanic has tools to work on cars. A carpenter cannot be without a hammer and nails. An accountant has pencils, erasers, a calculator, and tax charts to do her job. Being a professional Speed Cleaner also involves having the right tools to do the job fast and easy. Arming yourself to clean like a pro is surprisingly simple. Just assemble the following.

Basic Cleaners

Neutral Cleaner It is a misconception that cleaners must be harsh to be effective. Neutral pH cleaners are neither acidic nor alkaline. They are formulated with special blends of detergents that leave no harsh residue and are effective without harming humans or surfaces. They are one step above cleaning with water only because they add a bit more cleaning power. They are safe to use on many surfaces. Still, I recommend using only water on leather, ceramic tile, hardwood floors, laminate, brass, and marble.

TIP Buy a neutral cleaner at your local janitorial supplier, or you can make your own by mixing a few drops of mild dish detergent with a gallon of water.

Orange-Oil Cleaner Consider using an all-purpose orange-oil cleaner. Orange cleaners are degreasing agents, which makes them perfect for blinds, stoves, and other heavily soiled areas. I also use an orange-oil cleaner to remove gum, black grease, adhesive residue, and crayon drawings on the wall made by little artists. Best of all, orange-oil cleaners are nontoxic, and there are no harsh fumes. How can you be sure to buy a product that is made from real oranges when there are so many citrus-scented products on the market? Remember, buyer beware. Some "orange cleaners" are only orange-scented petroleum-based products. Look for labels that state that the product is made from pure oranges or orange oil. If the label does not specifically say the product contains orange oil, then it most likely does not.

★ My favorite cleaner is an oil squeezed from the rinds of more than 350 Valencia oranges. You can buy it ready to use or as a concentrate that you can dilute to the strength required for whatever you need to clean. An all-purpose citric orange cleaner is great for most household cleaning.

Glass Cleaner This is one of my favorite products because it shines surfaces to a sparkling sheen and also makes a great degreaser. It works well on stainless steel and appliances too. You can eliminate many products from your cleaning arsenal by purchasing a glass cleaner. My choice is always one of the antibacterial glass cleaners you can find on the grocery store shelves. The label should say it kills 99.9 percent of germs. I use it for so many things that taking it away would be like taking away a carpenter's hammer! Glass cleaners often contain ammonia, which is a diluted form of ammonium hydroxide and can be irritating to the respiratory system. Be sure to follow the directions to get the maximum safe antibacterial power.

> **TIP** Save money by purchasing glass cleaner with a sanitizer or disinfectant. You can clean and sanitize all at once, which will save you time and money.

Disinfectants, Sanitizers, and Germicidal Cleaners

Each plays a role in maintaining a healthy home, but which one should you use in which circumstance? There are important differences among these products that you need to know.

- ★ **Disinfectant** A chemical agent capable of destroying disease-causing pathogens or bacteria but not spores and not all viruses. Typically a disinfectant cleaner needs to sit on the surface for approximately 10 minutes to effectively disinfect it. Disinfectants can kill some viruses, which are considered to be living organisms. The main difference between a sanitizer and a disinfectant is a specified dilution; a disinfectant must have a higher kill capability for pathogenic bacteria.

- ★ **Sanitizer** Typically works to bring the number of microorganisms to a safe level. It kills the most common germs. Legally, a sanitizer must be capable of killing 99.9 percent of bacteria within 30 seconds. It can kill Salmonella, E. coli, staphylococcus (staph), and streptococcus (strep) on hard non-porous surfaces in 30 seconds. Sanitizers often contain alcohol. Sanitizers are not cleaners unless product labels specify this. Otherwise, a surface needs to be cleaned prior to sanitizing.

- ★ **Germicidal Cleaner** An antiseptic used to kill germs. Even your mouthwash can be considered germicidal. Germicides attack a specific part of the bacterial cell, killing or damaging it. A germicidal cleaner is a must to kill bacteria and other germs in kitchens and bathrooms. Sterilizing is the only way to kill all germs and spores.

True Cleaning Confessions

On my travels across the country, television news anchors frequently ask, "Are hand sanitizers good for us to use?" The debate on whether a sanitizer can reduce resistance to bacteria has excited a great deal of media attention. A study reported that using hand sanitizers can break down a child's resistance to bacteria. My response is that I would not recommend that anyone relax hygiene standards and handwashing frequency, both crucial to our overall health.

Non-abrasive Cream Cleansers

Cream cleansers are mildly gritty solutions that clean hard-to-remove soils without scratching surfaces. They are a good choice for those tougher spots. If you still like using a powder cleanser, only use it on non-scratchable surfaces. I have seen so many people use powder cleansers on scratchable surfaces and then have had to live with the scratches. Don't let that be you! Be particularly careful when cleaning glass cooktops. I highly recommend that you only use the new cream non-abrasive cooktop cleaners. These are formulated to clean, shine, and protect without scratching the surface. Use a soft sponge to apply the cleanser and to thoroughly rinse and dry the cooktop. Make sure that you always wait to clean a stove top until it is cool to the touch.

True Cleaning Confessions

After dinner at a friend's house I helped tidy the kitchen. I asked for a cloth to clean the countertops. She told me to use the sponge by the sink. I ran the sponge under water with a little dish detergent and the terrible smell made me realize the sponge was filled with bacteria. I told her it was time to throw the sponge away, and she quickly pulled out a fresh one. It's important to clean sponges after use in bleach or sanitizer. Rinse and dry thoroughly. Or microwave a damp sponge on high for 3 minutes to kill germs and bacteria. Discard sponges every other month, more often if they smell bad.

TIP Wash your hands and monitor your children's handwashing. Studies show that people claim they wash their hands every time they use the bathroom; but in reality only 67 percent of people actually do.

The Top Five Most Bacteria-Infested Places in Our Homes

Sponges The solution to keeping sponges clean is simple: Sanitize them or microwave them to kill bacteria.

Toothbrushes The situation with toothbrushes was the greatest shock to me. Every time we flush the toilet, water forms an aerosol that shoots a bacteria-laden mist of fecal matter up to 20 feet in the air. This mist settles on nearby sinks and countertops—as well as on whatever is on top of the counter, including toothbrushes. Teach family members to close the toilet lid before flushing. Another toothbrush issue is how to store them. If you keep them side by side in a holder or in the medicine cabinet, you provide a breeding ground for bacteria and viruses. Cold and flu viruses and the bacteria that cause gingivitis can travel from brush to brush.

Sinks It's important to disinfect sinks regularly. Kitchen sinks are where we wash raw meats. Meat juices cause bacterial growth.

Kitchen Countertops In the kitchen, countertops catch cooking splatters, grease, and who knows what from the hundreds of items we set on them. A swipe with a disinfectant wipe helps ensure cleanliness.

Wooden Cutting Boards Porous wood poses the risk of cross-contamination among different foods. Never use the same cutting board for raw meats and other foods; the wood absorbs meat blood, which breeds bacteria. Hand-wash cutting boards in warm soapy water immediately after preparing meats, and designate one cutting board for meat only. Another solution is to use plastic cutting boards that can be sterilized in the dishwasher.

Specialist Cleaning Kit

In my specialist cleaning kit are the products for those special cleaning jobs. Here are the products that can really save you time.

Multipurpose Cleaner Pick a cleaner that you can use on rust, soap scum, lime scale, iron, hard-water stains, or mineral deposits. Using one product is an important part of my "work smarter, not harder" philosophy. I really do not want to waste time and money purchasing four different products if it is possible to achieve the same cleaning with one cleaner. Read the label directions prior to using and make sure that you don't let a product sit on galvanized steel for long periods of time; it can pit the surface.

Disposable Wipes are great for people who can afford to buy them and get the most use from them. The neat thing about wipes is they are ready to use and can be used in a variety of cleaning tasks. No water or cleaner is required. Some wipes have disinfecting capabilities great for those quick toilet fixes. Other wipes are good for all-purpose cleaning.

Lemon Oil True lemon oil is made from lemons. Lemon oil is great for treating wood furniture (oak, pine, and others) when it is scratched or if it looks dry. It covers up the scratches and restores moisture. An application of lemon oil is especially helpful on wood that gets a great deal of heat (such as around dishwashers and floor vents) or foot traffic (around entry doors). As I suggested in chapter one, this product reduces soap scum on shower doors. A few words of caution: The lemon oil on the grocery store shelf contains petroleum distillates, so it is not something you want to leave in a combustible area.

Mineral Oil I love mineral oil. It's inexpensive, multipurpose, and it shines up dull stainless-steel sinks and sink fixtures. Food-quality mineral oil also can be used to safely moisturize wooden salad bowls and chopping blocks. It is colorless, tasteless, and some people even use it as a laxative. It can be purchased at supermarkets and pharmacies.

Enzyme Cleaner I like to have an enzyme cleaner on hand for pet accidents on the carpets and for urine odors around the toilets. Ordinary cleaners do not kill the bacteria which cause odor. Enzyme cleaners are various proteins found in plant and animal cells that act as organic catalysts in initiating or speeding up chemical reactions that usually become inactive or unstable. The bacteria left behind are what typically cause the odor in your home. Grout in the bathroom tends to be porous and traps the bacteria that can cause odor. Spraying an enzyme cleaner can neutralize that odor by digesting the bacteria. Enzyme cleaners can do this because they contain viable bacterial cultures similar to those in your digestive tract. These beneficial bacteria produce enzymes that digest organic substances. As a result they work great on vomit and urine. You also can use them on molds on tile grout, walls, and basement floors. For carpet spots, I like to use a syringe and inject the enzyme cleaner into the carpet pad. This is a very simple process, and the results are remarkable. Some enzyme cleaners recommend no rinsing so the cleaner can be absorbed into the surface. Look for enzyme cleaners at your local janitorial supply company.

TIP Use hydrogen peroxide to fight black mildew in the bathrooms and a pumice stone to help clean stubborn mineral and deposit stains in porcelain tubs, toilets, and sinks. Look for them at hardware stores or janitorial suppliers.

Stain-Removal Tips

★ **Alcohol** Soak in water or glycerin, and rinse in a vinegar and water solution.

★ **Blood** Rinse in cold water. For dried blood, try peroxide.

★ **Butter** Rub in a grease solvent followed by a one-hour soak in detergent before washing.

★ **Coffee** Blot with club soda or cold water.

★ **Gum** Dissolve it with peanut butter or an orange-oil cleaner.

★ **Ink** Apply a dollop of hair spray, scrub with a toothbrush, then launder.

★ **Ketchup** Wash in cold water and dish detergent, if caught fresh.

★ **Powdered Soft-Drink Mix** Rinse with water, if it's fresh. Launder with fabric-safe bleach.

★ **Sweat** Soak in white vinegar or laundry detergent. Launder.

★ **Lipstick** Rub in orange-oil cleaner.

★ **Pencil** Launder once with a strong detergent and a second time with ammonia. Rinse well. Repeat as needed.

Cleaning Cloths

My favorite cleaning cloth has always been and always will be a microfiber cloth. Microfiber cloths are the Cadillac of cleaning cloths, and they are revolutionizing the way we clean our homes. They cost more than conventional cloths, but they will save you time, eliminate cleaning products, and reduce the amount of muscle power you have to put into your cleaning.

Microfiber cleaning cloths have been used in Europe for years. Many large institutions, such as hospitals, hotels, and professional cleaning companies, use them daily. Microfiber has thousands of tiny, sharp edges that literally grab dirt, grime, mildew, and stains off surfaces. It locks them deep inside its tubular-shape star fibers like a magnet until they are rinsed off. The results are dramatic. Mirrors and patio doors that usually require extra work to remove the streaks and smears are no longer a problem. Microfiber cloths are nonstreaking and nonsmearing because they hold in the dirt. This means microfiber is an environmentally safe, economical way to clean almost anything.

Used dry, these cloths electrostatically pick up dust, surface dirt, lint, and hair. No more sneezing while dusting because the microfiber holds the dust particles in the tubular star fibers rather than just pushing them along the surface. The best part is you can clean without all the chemicals! I like to use my microfiber cloths half-damp with just plain water, half-dry to clean virtually any spill, stain, or dirt from most washable surfaces. Or, if you prefer, use microfiber cloths with your favorite cleaning solutions or polishing agents and you will have the most effective cleaning weapon against dirt that you can imagine! A microfiber cloth used as a buffing cloth makes sink fixtures and metal surfaces look shiny and polished.

Another advantage to microfiber is that it can absorb seven to ten times its weight in fluid! This makes it an exceptional spill grabber, often soaking up spills before they can become stains. I love to grab a microfiber cloth for carpet spills because it quickly absorbs all the liquid. Nine times out of 10, I can lift the stain by absorbing the excess liquid with a microfiber cloth, pouring a little cold water on the spot, and then firmly pressing a dry microfiber cloth on the spot to lift any remaining liquid. Voilà, it's gone! It works like magic.

Microfiber cloth is a blend of 80 percent polyester and 20 percent polyamide, split into microscopic wedge-shape microfilaments. It is a superior chemical-free, hypoallergenic textile. If you compare natural fiber and microfiber, you immediately see the difference. Fibers in natural materials, such as cotton or wool, have rounded edges, and their density is low because natural fibers are relatively thick. This means dirt and grime are just being pushed along the surface and not removed, leaving streaks and smears behind.

Microfiber cloths can be washed up to 500 times and still maintain their cleaning power! Just throw them in the washing machine or hand-wash them in mild soapy water, rinse, and hang or dry pop them in the dryer. The manufacturer recommends that you never use fabric softener, bleach, or dryer sheets when cleaning microfiber cloths. They also recommend that you not iron microfiber cloths (not that many people would iron their cleaning cloths, but just in case you wanted to, don't do it). You can find microfiber cloths at your local grocery store for about $3 to $5. You can also buy them on the Internet.

Should you throw away all your other cleaning cloths? No, you may need them to clean the oven, the garage, the patio furniture, barbecue grill, or the window screens. It's still OK to use cotton towels, old T-shirts, and blue shop towels for those really dirty jobs where you may want to throw the cloth away when you are done.

TIP Microfiber is 100 times thinner than a human hair and 10 times finer than silk, yet it is durable and aggressive, with more than 90,000 fibers per square inch. These fibers increase cleaning power and absorbency.

Cool Cleaning Tools

Black Ostrich Duster Use this for quick dusting of computers, TV screens, and knickknacks. I recommend black ostrich dusters for all your dusting jobs. Some people have debated the effectiveness of feather dusters. Cheap chicken feather dusters ($2) will not capture the dust as black ostrich feathers do. A black ostrich feather duster can cost you $5 to $20, depending on the size of the feathers. These dusters are available at home centers, mass merchandisers, and janitorial supply stores.

Cleaning Cloth Sturdy, thirsty, lint-free cloths, such as blue shop towels, bar towels, or cotton terrycloth towels (100-percent cotton is best), will come in handy for dirty cleaning jobs. After you wash and dry them, be sure to shake off the lint before using them to clean. (You don't want to clean up lint, which tends to transfer from the cloth to the surfaces.)

> **TIP** Don't launder cloths saturated with furniture polish or oil residues along with your all-purpose or glass cleaner cloths. Some oil stays in the cloths and leaves a hazy or streaky smear on windows and mirrors.

Microfiber Mop Imagine what this same fiber can do in a mop. Once you try one of these, you'll never go back to an old-fashioned one.

★ Ordinary household sponge mops quickly breed bacteria and germs if they are not washed, rinsed, and dried thoroughly after each use. String mops are prone to mold. In both cases, accumulated bacteria will be spread across your floors.

★ Those are good reasons for using microfiber or bucketless mops. As with mops that use disposable pads, microfiber and bucketless mops don't cover as wide an area as some old-fashioned sponge mops. But, in my experience, they work great for quick cleanups and spills. Both types are available at supermarkets, discount stores, and home centers. Microfiber mop pads are machine washable, which is a boon.

Dust Cloth, Treated Make your own treated dust cloth by spraying furniture polish on a microfiber, flannel, or other clean, absorbent fabric. Keep turning the cloth and squeezing it until the polish is evenly absorbed. Wash the cloth when it gets dirty and then re-treat it. This cloth is a weapon against dust, dust mites, and allergens that can give you itchy eyes and a runny nose. Under a microscope, more than 18,000 dust mites can be found in just 1 gram of dust. It's easy to see the health benefits of dusting your home!

Extension Duster Extension dusters are a necessity for cleaning hard-to-reach areas, such as behind washers, dryers, and headboards. My favorite can be bought at hardware stores for a respectable $5–$20, depending on the style you select. (See Laura's Favorite Products on pages 188–189.)

Telescopic Pole System Did you know more than 300 people die each year from injuries related to ladders? When added with minor injuries sustained from misuse, that's a total of 511,000 incidents per year. Sadly, a large number of these injuries could be prevented by following ladder safety guidelines. It makes perfect sense to stay off a ladder if there is an effective way to avoid it. It takes more time to clean when you have to get a ladder, set it up, climb up on it, and then put it back where it belongs. There goes 10 to 15 minutes of your cleaning time. Instead, try using a telescopic pole system. This is an extension pole with attachments, such as a black ostrich duster, a ceiling fan brush, and a lightbulb-changer tool. These poles come in lengths from 6-foot to 16-foot tall.

Grout Brushes Grout brushes reach into hard-to-reach cracks and crevices. They are like oversized toothbrushes with firmer bristles. You can buy them at janitorial suppliers or home stores for about $2. I also think it's a good idea to save old toothbrushes. Use a permanent marker to label them for their exact cleaning purpose. I use one each for kitchen sinks, countertop trim, toilets, shower doors, and wood surfaces.

Microfiber Cloths You just read about these—a revolutionary new type of cloth with a special weave and fiber that cleans without chemicals and absorbs practically like magic.

Plastic Putty Knife Use this to remove soap scum or mineral buildup on fiberglass showers. It is also great for removing hard candy or gum on no-wax floors. Just scrape away the grime with no fear of scratching your surface. It's a great option for windows, hardwood floors, and mirrors. You can find a putty knife in the paint section of any store. I use a 4-inch blade that covers a nice sized area.

Razor Blades Razor blades can be used to remove soap scum buildup, to clean sticky residue off glass, or for many other Spring Cleaning jobs. Be careful working on plastic surfaces and windows because they scratch easily. Keep the blade flat to the surface and work gently.

Squeegee Using a squeegee to clean your glass windows and patio doors reduces your cleaning time by 50 percent. I suggest that you purchase a professional squeegee with a stainless-steel handle and channel for around $15.

Tape or Gel Rollers These are great for picking up pet hair and human hair off furniture and other surfaces. I like sticky gel rollers better than tape rollers because you do not have to buy refills—simply rinse the roller under hot water.

Whisk Broom Use this to clean room edges, lampshades, heat vents, and doorjambs. It works great on steps, between railings, in corners, and on doors and hinges.

Toilet Brush My favorite toilet brush is a flushable brush that has the cleaner already in the pad. These are safe for all septic tanks, clean quickly, and take a two-step process down to one. The traditional choice is a brush with nylon bristles on a plastic wand. Stay away from the brushes with a metal head that can scratch your porcelain bowl or rust and leave stains after the brush wears down.

Hand-Held Steamer You can clean without harsh chemicals by using steam. This is great for people with asthma or allergies who are looking for natural cleaning methods. One of my favorite steam cleaners has attachments for floor cleaning and for getting into tight areas.

CHAPTER FIVE

Wet and Dry Work

Wet Work

Maid services break cleaning tasks down into two categories—wet work and dry work. Wet work is cleaning that requires water or a cleaning solution. Bathrooms and kitchens are two places we most often do wet work. In professional cleaning, the wet-work cleaner carries a caddy with the cleaning supplies. A two-person team is best; one person does the wet work, and the other does the dry work. If you have a family of four people, you can still break down the task appropriately. Keep in mind that to be a Speed Cleaning whiz, each person should have his or her own supplies in a bucket or caddy.

Wet Work Caddy List

- ★ Six to 10 cleaning cloths
- ★ Scrubby pad (such as those white or blue nylon scrub pads which won't scratch surfaces)
- ★ Scrub brush with nylon bristles
- ★ Microfiber flat mop
- ★ Old toothbrushes (one for toilets and one for sinks, each clearly marked)
- ★ Microfiber cloths
- ★ Grout brush
- ★ Toilet brush with nylon bristles or flushable pad toilet brush
- ★ Glass cleaner with disinfectant
- ★ All-purpose orange-oil cleaner/degreaser
- ★ Non-abrasive cream cleanser for delicate surfaces
- ★ Bathroom cleaner (lime scale, iron, rust, and mineral deposit remover and multipurpose cleaner)
- ★ Lemon oil (for shower doors and wood surfaces)
- ★ Dust cloth, treated (see chapter four)
- ★ Extension duster and telescopic pole system (for ceiling fans and skylights)

True Cleaning Confessions

In 1996, I taught training seminars at a local community college on how to operate a residential cleaning business. A lady called me, bragging that she was also a Speed Cleaning expert. She said that she had been cleaning for 15 years, retaining some of the same customers all those years. She asked me to come into one of her clients' homes and watch her work. Always willing to learn new methods, I took her up on her offer. One of the first things I noticed was that she used one cleaning cloth to clean the whole house. I questioned her about this and explained to her about the possibility of cross-contamination by using the same rag in the bathroom as well as in the kitchen. Your kids may try the same thing when they are cleaning. Tell them that it's important to use plenty of clean cloths, and give them a nice supply.

Wet Work Cleaning Tips

★ A damp microfiber cloth can clean 90 percent of most surfaces quickly and safely. Use a damp cloth by itself or with a mild, diluted dish detergent. The remaining surfaces that need disinfecting are in the kitchen and bathrooms.

★ Using fewer chemicals means less time, less waste, and greater safety. More is not better when it comes to spraying surfaces; more cleaning spray means more work for you!

★ Be careful not to overspray the cleaning chemical. Spraying your chemicals directly onto the cloth puts the cleaner where you want it and avoids buildup on surfaces.

★ Use a dry cloth after wet cleaning to buff and shine fixtures and chrome. This little trick is the difference between professional and non-professional cleaning. I like to use glass cleaner on sinks, fixtures, and shower doors, then buff.

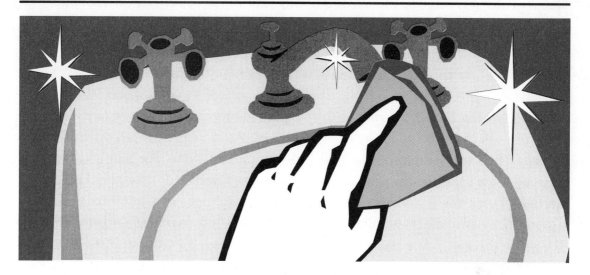

★ If the surface you are cleaning is particularly dirty, you may need to spray a little more heavily, let it sit a bit longer, and use an aggressive scrubby pad. Do not waste time using a cleaning cloth. If the surface you are cleaning is water-sensitive, spray the cleaner onto the cleaning cloth, rather than onto the surface, and use the cloth to wipe the surface.

★ Use microfiber cloths to save time and energy. You can clean wood, brass, painted surfaces, plastic, pictures, metal, glass, and mirrors in half the time.

★ Use toothbrushes for hard-to-reach cracks and crevices in wood tables, dressers, headboards, and desks. Keep these small brushes handy in your caddy.

★ For small floors, such as in a bathroom, use a damp cloth rather than a mop and bucket. I love the microfiber flat mops because they are fast and fit behind the toilet. Most no-wax floors require only water or a mild neutral cleaner.

> **TIP** Use 10 to 15 cleaning cloths to clean your home, depending on dirt level. In the bathroom alone you'll need one for mirrors, one for sinks and counters, one for the bathtub and shower, and one for walls and floors.

You can clean a bathroom in five minutes if you have faithfully performed a Deep Cleaning. It doesn't work if you haven't cleaned the bathroom in a year. Consider the five-minute routine as your weekly maintenance or quick spruce-up.

Start high at the bathroom mirror. Spray glass cleaner with disinfectant, buff dry, and then move on to spraying the fixtures, basin, and countertop. Buff fixtures. Then spray the tub, tile, and toilet, buff, and shine. For quick toilet cleaning try a toilet brush with flushable cleaner-filled pads. It works fast and sanitizes inside the toilet bowl in seconds! For the floors in a small bathroom, wipe with a damp cloth. A microfiber cloth avoids lint particles and smears. For a larger bathroom, use a flat mop. Your bathroom will be clean and disinfected in no time!

★ A cleaning cloth dampened with water cleans most surfaces safely. You should be able to refold your cloth eight times to a clean section as each section gets soiled.

★ A damp cloth followed immediately by a dry cloth works well on brass, walls, and wood. Take a clean cloth and dampen only half of it with water. Use the wet side to clean and the dry side to dry.

True Cleaning Confessions

I have been in all types of homes and met all types of people over the years. Some of the homes were comical in a messy sort of way. Viewing other people's homes has helped me relax about housekeeping. We have all heard the saying that a little dirt never killed anyone. A hardworking friend helps me find the comedic value in even the messiest of homes. She loved her clients and appreciated their business. Without dirt, she said, she would be out of a job. In the same way, when people find out what I do for a living, they sometimes apologize for the condition of their homes. I always say, "Don't worry, I love dirt! It's what keeps me in business!"

Dry Work

Now let's talk about dry work. This is cleaning such as sweeping, vacuuming, dusting, and emptying trash. Living rooms, family rooms, and bedrooms are three areas where we most often do dry work. In professional cleaning, the dry-work cleaner is the person who has a vacuum, a duster, cleaning cloths, and trash. Your dry work kit should be stocked with the following supplies.

Dry Work Caddy List

★ Vacuum (plus an extra bag and belt)

★ Black ostrich feather duster, extension duster, and telescopic pole extension system

★ Dry cloth treated with furniture polish

★ Trash bags

★ Microfiber cloths, lightly dampened with water, for spot-cleaning

★ Glass cleaner for bedroom mirrors and TV screens
(Don't spray the cleaner on these surfaces. Spray it on
a clean cloth and use the cloth to clean these surfaces.)

Does it matter which vacuum you use? Yes, if you have allergies or asthma. No, if dust in the home does not bother you and your home's indoor air quality is not a big issue.

Most people do not realize that conventional cloth or paper vacuum bags may pick up only 30 percent of the dirt from carpets and blow 70 percent of the fine dust back into the air. If you have been wondering why your home looks dusty again in a few hours, there's your answer. If you live in a rural area, such as with Arizona's fine red dust, then you know very well what I am talking about.

High Efficiency Particulate Air (HEPA) vacuums are everywhere. The Institute of Environmental Science requires that a Certified HEPA media filter capture a minimum of 99.97 percent of contaminants at least 0.3 microns in size. This shows why they are important when considering a new vacuum cleaner purchase or an air-filtration system for your home.

There are many HEPA media filters on the market. A HEPA filter can capture invisible air allergens and contain them in the vacuum, stopping the airborne allergens being blown back into the air and improving the quality of the air you breathe.

Why do microns matter? A micron is one-millionth of a meter, or about $\frac{1}{70}$ the thickness of a human hair. Dust particles less than 10 microns are invisible to the human eye. Traditional cleaning methods capture the visible dirt in cloth or paper vacuum bags. Today's homeowners are concerned about what they breathe and are looking at vacuums that reduce airborne dust.

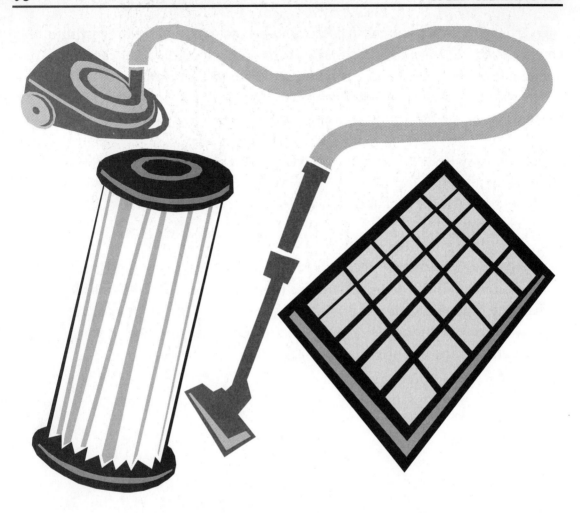

You have two choices that will improve particle containment:

★ Purchase Ultra Low Penetration Air (ULPA) filters. These are a bit more costly than standard microfilter vacuum bags but provide the highest level of reduction of particulate release.

★ Purchase a vacuum with a High Efficiency Particulate Air (HEPA) filter.

Both ULPA and HEPA filters typically are installed as secondary filters. The primary filter captures the larger visible dust.

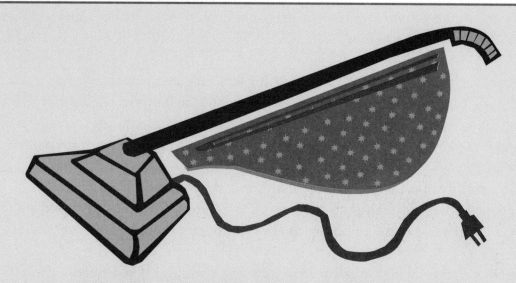

How Do I Know If I Need a New Vacuum?

★ If your children are playing tic-tac-toe or writing their names with their fingers on the dust on your coffee tables.

★ If you sneeze up a dust ball every time you walk into your home.

★ If your visitors ask for a towel before they sit on your furniture.

Test Your Vacuum for Quality Cleaning

★ If you can see tiny particles of dust, called *motes,* floating around in the sunlight, your vacuum is blowing dust.

★ If you slap your upholstered furniture and see dust motes, the likely culprit is a vacuum that has been adding airborne dust.

★ If you are changing your vacuum's belts every few months it's time for a new vacuum. The newest upright vacuums use belts similar to automotive timing belts—they are geared and sprocketed so they don't slip or stretch and seldom wear out.

It is easy to be overwhelmed by the astounding number of models and features available. Here's some help.

1. **How much can you afford to spend?** A good vacuum cleaner may run $200 to $400. If air quality is not important, a $69 vacuum from a big-box store works well. These are a good choice for poor college students who never change the vacuum bags until they explode, usually after the last dorm party!

2. **Do amps matter?** Amp is short for ampere, a measure of electric current. Vacuum cleaners have ratings from 5 amps to 12 amps. Higher amperage doesn't always mean more cleaning power; airflow is a better measure of effectiveness.

3. **What provides a high-quality, low-emission cleaning?** If you need a good vacuum that emits fewer airborne particulates, go with one that offers four-level filtration and uses microfilters and a HEPA filter.

4. **How important is airflow?** Airflow and suction are created by the vacuum's motor fan. Airflow is usually measured in cubic feet per minute (cfm). Suction created by a vacuum cleaner's rotating fan creates a stream of air. Suction will be stronger or weaker depending on the power of the fan, blockage of the air passage, and the size of the intake opening. I recommend vacuums that are approved by the Carpet and Rug Institute (CRI). To qualify for a CRI green label, a vacuum undergoes a three-part performance test. For more information about CRI testing, go to *www.carpet-rug.com.*

5. **Do you need one motor or two?** Single-motor uprights do not clean as well as double-motor units. A two-motor upright has separate motors to turn the beater brush and create suction. The downside of a two-motor unit is that it is heavier; many homeowners want lightweight units.

6. **How much noise can you tolerate?** Many people are concerned about on noise. To respond to this concern, some models have insulated materials around the motors to make them quieter.

True Cleaning Confessions

I like backpack-style vacuums for efficiency, comfort, and safety. For big jobs, a backpack vacuum reduces cleaning time. It's ergonomically designed for ease of use. You can get models that have attachments that ride on the vacuum or clip on a waist belt. I'm able to put my cleaning tools and cloths on my belt and multitask: I can dust and vacuum in one complete movement throughout a room. For quick jobs, I prefer a cordless vacuum with a simple dirt tray for easy emptying. One of my favorite cordless vacuums cleans carpets, hardwood floors, and edges quickly and easily. If you are looking for an inexpensive vacuum that is cordless, efficient, does not require bags, and is easy for small children to use, then a cordless stick vacuum is for you.

CHAPTER SIX

Speed Cleaning Room by Room

Speed Clean Your Kitchen

The kitchen often is called the heart of the home. In many homes, it is the family gathering space as well as the food preparation place. So, of course, you want it to be clean and pleasant; but, unfortunately, because of its heavy use, it seldom meets this standard. But take heart! You can Speed Clean the kitchen and make it the healthy place it should be.

Time was that it seemed to take forever to clean the kitchen. That's no longer the case. By using Speed Cleaning techniques, you can be out of the kitchen in no time.

OLD-FASHIONED METHOD: **45 minutes**
SPEED CLEANING METHOD: **20 minutes**

Kitchen Speed Cleaning Supplies

- ★ Glass cleaner formulated with a disinfectant, for countertops and the outsides of appliances
- ★ Microfiber cloths
- ★ Scrub pad
- ★ All-purpose orange-oil cleaner for cleaning and degreasing
- ★ Multipurpose cleaner for lime, rust, scale, and stains around the sink fixtures
- ★ Toothbrush for sinks, fixtures, and metal trim around sink
- ★ An extended-reach duster and telescopic pole extension system (for getting under the refrigerator and into gaps between cabinets and walls)
- ★ Non-abrasive cream cleanser
- ★ Microfiber flat mop
- ★ Vacuum

Deep Cleaning Supplies

All of the above, plus
- ★ Lemon oil for dry woodwork or porous oak cabinetry
- ★ Mineral oil for shining stainless-steel sinks

REMEMBER THE FOUR BASIC TECHNIQUES
1) Be organized: Have all your supplies on or near you.
2) Clean from top to bottom.
3) Work the room in a circle. Finish one room at a time.
4) Don't clean what's already clean.

Step 1

Enter the kitchen with your duster and your glass cleaner in hand and have both a damp and a dry cloth over your shoulder. Start with high-dusting, paying attention to walls and corners, ceilings, and door and window frames. Use the water-dampened cloth to spot-clean ledges, walls, and dusty door frames as you work around the room. Now move downward to mid-dusting. Dust pictures and bookshelves with a treated dust cloth or ostrich duster. You can spray sanitizer on a second damp cloth for wiping switchplates, refrigerator handles, and cabinet knobs. Then do your low-dusting of baseboards and floors. Make every step and every movement count to increase your speed. Spray glass cleaner onto a cloth to wipe glass surfaces you pass. Buff glass, chrome, and stainless steel with a dry cloth.

Step 2

Now do the wet work. Put your supply caddy on the kitchen counter. Start cleaning at the corner of the room where the refrigerator is. Using the glass cleaner or all-purpose orange-oil cleaner, a damp cloth, and a dry cloth, spray and wipe where it's dirty only.

Clean the refrigerator handle each time you clean; that is one of the most bacteria-infested places in the entire kitchen! I also recommend spraying disinfectant on the water dispenser in your refrigerator door and washing the drip plate weekly. Clean the front and the sides of the refrigerator, the microwave, the stove, and the cooktop only where they are dirty. For coffee or juice stains on the counter, use a dab of cream cleanser and a damp cloth on the spot only. Spray and wipe the counters with glass cleaner. Continue to work your way around the room in a circle.

If the sink is not dirty, spray it with a glass cleaner containing a disinfectant that kills 99.9 percent of household germs and buff it with the dry cloth until it shines. If the sink has buildup from hard water, use lime-scale remover. Use a toothbrush or scrub pad to clean behind the faucet fixture base. For the black marks and scratches on porcelain sinks that come from pots and pans, use a generous amount of cream cleanser on a scrub pad. The marks and scratches will disappear!

As you are working your way around the kitchen, spray the cabinets with orange-oil cleaner and wipe them dry. Orange-oil cleaner works well on greasy fingerprints around the cabinet handles.

> **TIP** If you have wooden kitchen cabinets, use a damp cloth for routine cleaning. For dry or scratched wooden cabinets or baseboards, clean with a damp cloth and then treat them with lemon oil.

Step 3

Finally, sweep or vacuum the floor. Start in the furthermost corner and work your way out of the room. Mop or hand-wash the floor with a neutral cleaner. Mix your cleaning solution with lukewarm water because full-strength cleaners and hot water break down the floor's finish.

Deep Cleaning Tasks

★ **Clean behind and underneath the refrigerator/freezer.** Use an extended-reach duster. Doing this once a month is sufficient, but if you do this weekly, all the better.

★ **Clean the inside of the refrigerator and the freezer.** Use warm soapy water. A toothbrush is the perfect tool to clean those rubber seals and grooves.

★ **Clean the inside of the oven.** For a self-cleaning oven, follow the manufacturer's directions. Sometimes there is an odor, so turn on the exhaust fan or open a window. For regular ovens, buy professional strength oven cleaner from a janitorial supplier. Spray it on, wait 10 minutes, and wipe the oven clean. The professional-strength cleaner has no harsh smell and works quickly.

★ **Polish cabinets.** Apply lemon oil to scratched or dry wood.

★ **Shine sinks.** Use mineral oil to shine a stainless steel sink.

★ **Clean cutting boards.** Sanitize wooden cutting boards and chopping blocks, then use mineral oil to moisturize them.

Quick Tips for the Kitchen's Trouble Areas

★ **Greasy cabinets** Microwave your cloth until it is hot. Wear heat-resistant gloves. (There are gloves on the market that provide protection from temperatures up to 600 degrees.) Spray surfaces with orange-oil cleaner. Use the hot cloth to wipe the cabinets.

★ **Dirty sink stoppers and rubber mats** Put in dishwasher; add $1/4$ cup bleach instead of dishwashing detergent.

★ **Grease on backsplash by kitchen stove** Try using cloth heated in the microwave and an orange-oil cleaner or a degreaser. If you can scrape the buildup with a fingernail, first use a plastic putty knife to remove the excess, then do a Deep Clean.

True Cleaning Confessions

Are your kitchen sinks cleaner than your toilets? You would be better off making a ham and cheese sandwich on the average toilet seat than in a kitchen sink, according to a recent study. When 14 different surfaces were tested, the most germs were found in the kitchen—on sponges, dishcloths, and sinks—and the fewest on toilet seats. Can you imagine your spouse saying, "Honey, can you bring me the mayo? I need to hurry up and make my sandwich on the toilet seat before one of the kids bursts in to use the bathroom!" Far-fetched? In the study, toilets did not even make the Top 5 list.

A microbiologist conducted a study in 15 typical homes over $7\frac{1}{2}$ months. Over that time period, he counted kitchen and bathroom germs weekly. He called the highest bacteria count areas hot zones. The hot zones were considered to be the main transfer areas for illness-causing germs.

The five kitchen hot zones
1. Sponges and dishcloths
2. Kitchen sinks and drain areas
3. Kitchen faucet handles
4. Cutting boards
5. Refrigerator handles

You have heard of rabbits multiplying fast, but there are not many things that can multiply as rapidly as bacteria, which can double its number in just 20 minutes. This means that bacterium on a kitchen countertop can multiply to more than 34 billion in just 12 hours.

You can see the importance of proper disinfecting. We are the germ fighters, grime warriors, and health monitors of the home. Sponges and dishcloths are the main culprits, with more than 7 billion bacteria per average-sized sponge. Kitchen faucet handles netted an average of 229,000 germs per square inch, and cutting boards ended up with an average of 62,000 bacteria per square inch.

The Food and Drug Administration (FDA) does not provide an exact number of bacteria it takes to make humans sick. But think about how many times you've started off the day feeling great and ended up with a bad headache, nausea, or diarrhea. Bacteria such as E. coli and salmonella cause foodborne illnesses. We may not be able to pinpoint where or why we've become ill, but the source could be the sandwich we made on the kitchen counter. The best approach is proper daily cleaning of the five hot zones.

Sterilize sponges. These become breeding grounds for bacteria trapped in their hollows. Boil sponges for three minutes to sterilize them. You also can put damp sponges in the microwave for three minutes on high; dry sponges can catch fire. (This works on cellulose sponges only; the microwave will destroy natural sponges.) Maintain sponges by cleaning them after each and every use. Two minutes of soaking in soap and hot water can remove about 97 percent of the bacteria. You also can clean them with a sanitizer product, disinfectant, or by soaking them for a few minutes in bleach and water. (Don't leave sponges too long in bleach solution or they'll disintegrate.)

Use clean dishcloths. Make it a habit to put a fresh one out daily. Any time you clean up meat drippings and juices, change the cloth immediately.

Sanitize sinks and faucets. This is where we put our road kill, according to one microbe hunter. The main culprit: meat juices that leak out of packages or run into the sink when you're rinsing poultry. These juices allow salmonella to breed. Clean sinks and counters after exposing them to raw meats. A solution of bleach and water, or a disinfectant wipe, will do the job.

Disinfect cutting boards. It's best to stay away from wood cutting boards and instead use non-porous plastic ones. Disinfect them with bleach or put in your automatic dishwasher to eliminate the bacteria that can cause foodborne illnesses.

Sanitize the refrigerator handle. This is one of the easiest things to overlook but also is one of the dirtiest places in our kitchens. A sanitizer kills 99 percent of household germs.

Speed Clean Your Bathroom

A luxurious soak in the bathtub, or even a quick hot shower, is much more pleasurable in a sparkling clean bathroom. But bathrooms don't stay tidy or sanitary for long, especially when you have kids splashing about (and don't even mention boys and toilets!). Cleaning this room doesn't have to be dreaded drudgery if you know how to Speed Clean. You should do one deep clean prior to Speed Cleaning your bathroom.

OLD-FASHIONED METHOD: **25 minutes**
SPEED CLEAN METHOD: **10 minutes or less**

Bathroom Speed Cleaning Supplies

- ★ Glass cleaner formulated with a disinfectant antibacterial cleaner
- ★ Cleaning cloths
- ★ Scrub pad
- ★ All-purpose orange-oil cleaner
- ★ Toothbrushes for sinks and toilets
- ★ Extension duster and telescopic pole extension system
- ★ Cream cleanser
- ★ Toilet brush
- ★ Disinfectant cleaner
- ★ Toilet bowl cleaner

Deep Cleaning Supplies

- ★ Powerful bathroom cleaner to remove lime, water spots, mineral deposits, scale, rust, and iron or hard-water stains
- ★ Lemon oil
- ★ Mineral oil
- ★ Peroxide or bleach for black mildew
- ★ Pumice stone

Step 1

When you first walk into the room, add disinfectant cleaner or toilet bowl cleaner to the inside of the bowl. Dust all the high spots with a damp microfiber cloth or an extension duster. This high-dusting should include the lights above the vanity, the top of the shower partition, and shelves. Keep refolding your cloth to the clean side. Next, use glass cleaner on the bathroom mirror, counters, and sink fixtures. Remember to Speed Clean by spraying only the dirty areas. Let the disinfectant sit on the surfaces as recommended by the manufacturer to get the full disinfecting benefit—45 seconds to 10 minutes. You also can use sanitizing wipes as a timesaver. Finally, buff the surfaces with a dry cloth.

> **TIP** To clean lightbulbs, make sure they are cool
> to the touch and gently wipe them with a dry cloth.

Step 2

Check the shower, tub, tile, and any sliding doors for mildew, soap scum, and mineral deposits. Spray the shower with all-purpose bathroom cleaner, rub it in, rinse, and wipe dry. For mold removal, spray full-strength peroxide, leave it on the surface three to five minutes, and then scrub with a grout brush. Reapply peroxide as needed. If the tub is dirty, start at the top and work your way around the tub in a circle using cream cleanser and an aggressive scrub pad or scrub brush. Rinse well. Use a toothbrush to clean the shower door tracks and around the shower fixtures. Wipe the showerhead and the shower doors. If the doors have a white, chalky look from mineral-scale buildup, clean with lime remover on a scrub pad and rinse well. Apply lemon oil as explained in chapter one. This will freshen the bathroom and repel soap-scum buildup, making future cleaning easier. Do this twice a month.

Step 3

Now for everyone's favorite—toilet cleaning. A survey showed 48 percent of people responding consider the toilet to be the worst cleaning chore. But it can be so simple to clean! In Step 1, you poured cleaner into the bowl. Most toilet cleaners recommend allowing them to sit for 10 minutes to disinfect. Now you can finish cleaning. Start at the top of the toilet tank. Spray disinfectant cleaner on the tank lid, front, sides, handle, seat (both bottom and top), hinges, base, and anchor bolts. Using a disposable cleaning cloth, wipe down all of these surfaces. Scrub the inside of the toilet with a plastic bowl brush. Or you can use a disposable brush. If you have mineral-scale buildup in the toilet, use a pumice stone to remove it. Flush the toilet and wipe the entire toilet again with a dry cloth.

> **TIP** Flush the toilet twice if you have household pets
> to prevent accidental ingestion of chemicals.

Step 4

In a small bathroom, hand-wash the floor. Use a neutral cleaning solution or plain warm water to clean and preserve the finish on no-wax floors. Use an all-purpose or disinfectant cleaner and a scrub brush for vinyl floors that are heavily soiled. An enzyme cleaner is good for stains or odors around the base of the toilet. If you prefer a mop, you can use one of the bucketless mops for fast cleanup. Cleaning a small bathroom floor should only take one minute. For larger bathrooms, a flat mop with a microfiber pad works well.

Additional Tasks for Deep Cleaning

If your bathroom has not been cleaned for a while, you will have to attack black mold, rust spots, and soap scum. You will be amazed how clean your bathroom stays for longer periods of time. For floors with built-up dirt, try a scrub brush on a pole. You can buy one at a janitorial supplier, hardware store, or home center. (Look in the Yellow Pages under Janitorial Suppliers.) Often these firm brushes on a broom-style handle are referred to as deck brushes. These tools make it fast and easy to scrub textured vinyl or no-wax floors and also work well on tile to clean the grout.

Speed Clean Your Living Room

Think about it: The living room is where you want to live, not be mired in chores. In some homes, this is the room reserved for visitors; in others, it is where the family relaxes. Yet it often becomes a catchall for clutter: Magazines, toys and games, remote controls for the entertainment system—all of these items get strewn. Even if the room is reserved for entertaining guests, it will accumulate dust. Routinely cleaning this room turns it back into the retreat it is meant to be.

OLD-FASHIONED METHOD: **15 minutes**
SPEED CLEAN METHOD: **10 minutes**

Living Room Speed Cleaning Supplies

★ Glass cleaner
★ Dry microfiber cloth
★ Damp microfiber cloths
★ Treated dust cloth
★ Lemon oil
★ Black ostrich feather duster
★ Extension duster and telescopic pole system
★ Vacuum cleaner
★ Whisk broom

Deep Cleaning Supplies

★ Lemon oil
★ Carpet and upholstery cleaner

Step 1

Check the room to determine the degree of cleaning it needs. First, tidy the room. A three-minute pickup makes the rest of the job much easier. Pick up out-of-place items, such as dishes, newspapers, toys, and books. Empty the trash cans and ashtrays. Don't worry about putting everything away at this point. Toss the picked-up items in a laundry basket and stash it in a closet. When and if family members start asking for their lost stuff, let them sift through the basket for it. This may cure them of leaving things scattered around the house!

Step 2

Start by high-dusting light fixtures, ceilings, corners, bookshelves, and ledges. Use a feather duster for light dust, such as on pictures, lampshades, knickknacks, and electronic entertainment equipment. If you need to spot-clean, spray glass cleaner onto a cloth and wipe away the marks. Have a clean microfiber cloth that is half-dry and half-dampened with water over your shoulder so as you

move around the room you can wipe off spots on walls, leather furniture, brass lamps, and the like. You can safely dust every surface in the room with a damp microfiber cloth. Move on to mid-dusting and surface cleaning in one sweeping motion around the room.

One of the coolest cleaning tools I have ever used is a plastic whisk broom that cost less than $3. It has been a lifesaver. It works great for brushing up the dirt and lint that collects on carpets along the baseboard. Some vacuums cannot get into those tight spaces. You also can use a whisk broom to remove crumbs from under couch cushions, dust pleated lampshades, and clean cobwebs, doorjambs, and vents. A handy whisk broom is easier and quicker than putting attachments on your upright vacuum. I stick mine in my back pocket or waistband so it's always with me when I need it. As you vacuum, you now will be able to pick up the dust, crumbs, and debris that you have whisked out of the crevices.

Step 3

Time to vacuum Most people have no organized, systematic approach to vacuuming. Short strokes in no particular pattern make vacuuming a long and tedious chore. You need an organized approach. To clean like a professional, throw the vacuum cord over your shoulder. Use your free hand to hold the cord so you can fling it behind you as you back up. This way you have control over the cord to avoid stepping on it or running over it. Push the vacuum all the way up one side of the room. Turn and walk back down the next row. Vacuuming in rows is quick and covers the widest area. Back out of the room to prevent footprints in carpeting that shows tracks. If you have a good-quality vacuum, and use it once a week, one pass should be enough. If you allow shoes to be worn indoors, or if you have pets, it may take two or three passes with the vacuum to clean the carpet.

Vacuum the high-traffic areas each time. You can catch the corners and edges of the room once or twice a month. If you have asthma or allergies in your family, it would be wise to vacuum daily or weekly, depending on the severity of the problem, with a HEPA media filter.

Quick Tips

★ **Spot vacuum only high-traffic areas.** This will save you time and energy and is a quick Spruce-Up if you have unexpected company.

★ **Use a damp cloth treated with leather polish** to clean leather furniture according to manufacturer's recommendations.

True Cleaning Confessions

When I started cleaning professionally in 1990, most people had formal living rooms. The funny thing was no one ever sat in a formal living room; they were basically for show. Rooms like that were the easiest to clean. There was little dust, and many times there wasn't even a footprint on the carpet. It's safe to apply the "don't clean what's already clean" principle in rooms like this. A light dusting of the horizontal surfaces and a spot vacuuming should be sufficient. Remember, if it looks good and smells good, the general perception is that it must be clean!

Additional Tasks for Deep Cleaning

★ Move the furniture and vacuum underneath it.

★ Lift the couch cushions and whisk or vacuum crumbs.
   It's "finders keepers" if you come across money!

★ Use enzyme cleaners on pet stains or odor in carpets.

★ Use a spray air-neutralizer to remove smoke or cigarette odors.

★ Clean the miniblinds, ceiling fan blades, and walls with an
   all-purpose cleaner.

★ Clean the carpet and upholstery as necessary. You can purchase
   carpet and upholstery cleaner at the supermarket. For larger
   carpet areas, you can rent a carpet-cleaning machine at grocery
   stores, discount stores, and hardware stores. Also purchase a
   carpet and upholstery protector spray. Apply it each time you
   deep clean.

★ Work lemon oil into wood surfaces that look dry or scratched.

★ Fill in scratches on furniture using stain-marking pens.

TIP Use a whisk broom around carpet edges and baseboards and to remove
crumbs under couch cushions, dust pleated lampshades, clear cobwebs, and
sweep doorjambs and vents.

TIP To clean like a professional, throw the vacuum cord over your shoulder.
Use your free hand to control the cord while vacuuming.

TIP Vacuuming in rows is quick and covers the widest area.

Speed Clean Your Bedroom

On average, your bedroom is where you spend one-third of your day! It is important to keep it clean, as it is where you tend to spend the majority of your day and it's where you sleep at night. A clean bedroom is important to people who suffer from allergies and asthma. Many people with allergies are amazed at how bad their symptoms are while in the bedroom.

OLD-FASHIONED METHOD: **20 minutes**
SPEED CLEAN METHOD: **10 minutes**

Bedroom Speed Cleaning Supplies

- ★ Treated dust cloth
- ★ Furniture polish
- ★ Ostrich feather duster
- ★ Extension duster
- ★ Vacuum cleaner
- ★ Whisk broom
- ★ Damp microfiber cloth
- ★ Dry microfiber cloth
- ★ Glass cleaner

Deep Cleaning Supplies

- ★ Telescopic pole system for cleaning ceiling fan
- ★ Skylight or recessed-ceiling duster on extension pole

Step 1

Start by tidying the room, emptying trash cans, and picking up clothes, shoes, and toys. Change the bed linens if needed. Wash bedding once a week. For households with allergy sufferers, you can use a laundry additive that eliminates dust mites.

Step 2

Dust all the high spots Start with ceilings, corners, bookshelves, and ledges. With a damp cloth, spot-clean walls, headboards, lamps, etc., as you move around the room. Dust behind dressers or headboards with the extension duster. Use the feather duster for lampshades, knickknacks, and pictures. Have your glass cleaner and a dry cloth ready for surfaces that need cleaning. Use a treated dust cloth on wood surfaces and windowsills. Use your whisk broom on hard-to-reach places, such as the carpet edges, pleated lampshades, and vents.

Step 3

Vacuum high-traffic areas Vacuum or whisk the corners and edges once or twice a month or as needed (see p. 63). At least once a month, hit that depository of dust under the bed. Most upright vacuums have handles that go down to the floor if you hold in the release button. For hardwood floors, use a microfiber duster.

Health Alert If you suffer from allergies or asthma, do a detailed cleaning each time. Encase mattresses and pillowcases in allergen-protective covers, vacuum with a HEPA or high-efficiency filter vacuum, and wash bedding in hot water (at least 130 degrees) each week. If your water heater is not set that high, purchase the dust mite laundry additive. Visit my website for questions regarding this topic at *www.healthyhousekeeper.com.*

> **TIP** Wash the bedding once a week in water that is 130 degrees or hotter. It is important for people suffering from allergies. For others who do not want to use water temperatures that high, try a dust-mite laundry additive that eliminates dust mites in the washer. It's available on the Internet.

Additional Tasks for Deep Cleaning

★ Turn the mattress and vacuum it with a HEPA vacuum.

★ Clean the things you don't regularly wash, such as dust ruffles, pillows, and curtains.

★ Move the furniture and vacuum underneath it.

True Cleaning Confessions

Here is a story to which I think every parent can relate. My mother was a single mom who had to raise seven children. Although her stress had to be intense at times, she came from a family of 11 children and took a completely different approach. My mother established a "clean before you play" rule. During the summer, there was always something going on in our neighborhood that attracted kids. Freeze tag, hide and seek, and going to the local swimming pool filled our days. My mom was bombarded daily with her seven children asking to go here, there, and everywhere. Mom said, "OK, before you go you have to do these chores...." At first we complained, but as we got used to it, we hurried to do our tasks. Sometimes my friends helped me so I could leave sooner! However, don't let a fairy-tale image pop into your head about my family; we were far from perfect when it came to cleaning—especially in our bedrooms. My brothers and sisters and I were notorious for hiding stuff under our beds and shoving junk into our closets and drawers to make our rooms look clean. My sisters and I would try on five different outfits in the morning but were too lazy to hang up all the clothes afterward.

CHAPTER SEVEN

Speed Clean Your Laundry Room

Cleaning a room that's intended for cleaning might seem an odd concept, but consider what this space goes through. Laundry rooms can get extremely dusty from dryer lint floating in the air. Water drips as laundry is moved from washer to dryer, the wet floor is walked on, and so the floor gets dirty. Perhaps pets eat or sleep in this room. A round of Speed Cleaning keeps the laundry area ready for service.

OLD-FASHIONED METHOD: **10 minutes**
SPEED CLEAN METHOD: **5 minutes**

Laundry Room Speed Cleaning Supplies

- ★ Extension duster
- ★ Glass cleaner
- ★ Damp microfiber cloth
- ★ Dry microfiber cloth
- ★ Microfiber mop

Step 1

High-dust with an extension duster. Mid-dust and clean shelves, tables, and windowsills with a damp cloth. Also use a damp cloth to clean light switchplates and remove spots on the walls. Low-dust, especially behind the washer and dryer, using an extension duster. Wipe up laundry detergent spills.

Step 2

Wipe the front and the sides of appliances. Clean the washer and dryer with glass cleaner sprayed on a cloth. Buff them until they shine.

Step 3

Sweep or vacuum the floor and then mop. If you want to clean the floor under the washer and dryer, dip your extension duster into warm water, wring it out, place it back on the handle, and use it to clean those hard-to-reach places. When done, remove the duster from the handle and toss it in the washing machine.

True Cleaning Confessions

Each month I do a radio interview with WBCL Fort Wayne, Indiana, called *Rise and Shine with Phil Reaser.* One day he called me and said he'd had a fire in the clothes dryer. The odd thing was that both he and his wife cleaned the lint trap regularly. As it turned out, a $1/4$ inch blanket of lint had built up inside the dryer base (after eight years of use). When the pilot light ignited the gas, it also ignited that layer of lint. It gave him a scare—me too. I went to the U.S. Consumer Product Safety Commission website and found out that in 2003 there were 15,600 dryer fires, 370 deaths and injuries, and damage estimated at $75.4 million. I yanked out my vacuum and duster and started cleaning my clothes dryer. You can avoid being one of these statistics. In addition to cleaning the filter each time you use the machine, cleaning the lint out of the exhaust pipe and checking the drum once a year reduce chances of a dryer fire, result in faster drying times, and save energy.

Dryer Safety Tips:

★ Clean the lint filter with each use.

★ Vacuum inside your dryer vent periodically.

★ Take off the front panel and vacuum around the vent and exhaust areas.

★ Remove lint buildup on the heater housing; it can ignite if there is a blocked exhaust vent or a failed thermostat.

★ Remove lint near the heater intake; it has the potential to ignite from the spark if the thermostat switches the element off.

★ For more fire safety information, see the U.S. Fire Administration website at *www.usfa.fema.gov/public/factsheets/safety.shtm.*

True Cleaning Confessions

The one area in my home that gets away from me is the laundry room. One moment, it looks great, then the next there are wet dish towels stacked on the washer, and my ironing board is piled with clothes. Pairing socks is the worst! Folding has to wait until I find the time. I wish I could blame the size of the room or the lack of storage space. But there are answers: Take advantage of inexpensive organizing tools, such as soft plastic disks that slide onto pairs of socks to keep them from separating in the washer (or being eaten by the dryer!). But the No. 1 rule is: Teach your family members, even the children, to wash, hang, and fold their own clothes.

Outfitting the Laundry Room

If you have a choice and the space, an organized laundry room helps remove stress from your life. Let's face it: We need clean clothes every day. Mothers in large families tell me that every day is wash day.

A laundry room off the kitchen has been a gift to many households. Newer homes offer even more choices: You can put a laundry room upstairs by the bedrooms or insert a mini laundry room into a large closet. Kitchen installation, for example, makes sense if you do laundry along with other chores. Instead of the traditional laundry room, a washer, dryer, and utility supply closet near the bedrooms may save steps for you.

What laundry location works best for you? Locating the washer and dryer in the basement means extra steps, but this arrangement frees up valuable upstairs space. Spills, splashes, or overflow normally do less damage in a basement. Upstairs, a leak could damage walls, flooring, and the ceiling below. If you install a washing machine near your main living area, add an emergency shut-off valve and regularly check hose connections. Among the considerations when deciding where to put a laundry room are plumbing and wiring. Washers require drains and hot and cold water lines. Gas dryers need a gas supply line and a maximum of 50 feet of venting to the outside. Electric dryers require 120-volt circuits. Some models condense moisture into a drip pan without venting. Washers and gas dryers require 20-amp small-appliance circuits. Units must be on independent, grounded circuits.

Another important point is storage space. Install shelving near the washer to keep supplies handy. Bleach and other laundry products are dangerous to young children, so place them on shelves well out of the reach of children. (For more on bleach storage, see chapter four.) If possible, install a childproof lockable cabinet. Install a rack to hang clothes that drip-dry, or buy a double-tier clothes rack on wheels or casters. For tight spaces, use wooden, metal, or plastic drying racks. Purchase drying racks for sweaters and knits that must be air-dried while flat and place them on the top of the washing machine, dryer, or in a bathtub if drying space is limited. Some clothes dryers have drying shelves in cabinets that sit atop the machine and use vented air to dry delicate items.

Uniform, glare-free lighting is important in the laundry room to thoroughly inspect, sort, and fold clothes. Compact fluorescent bulbs illuminate without adding heat. Some wall-mounted ironing boards include a built-in task light.

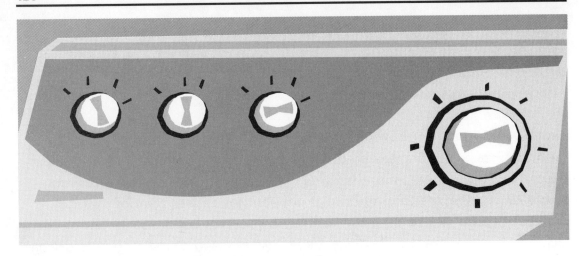

Washers and Dryers

Washers and dryers measure from 24 to 33 inches wide. For loading and unloading, allow 36 inches in front of a washer, 42 inches for a dryer. Measurements differ for front-loading models. Stacked units occupy less than 33 square inches of floor space and are accessible to people who have difficulty bending or stooping; front-loaders are more accessible to wheelchair users. Install machines about 15 inches off the floor to make loading and unloading more comfortable.

Selecting a Washer

Consider both capacity and loading type. Capacity depends on the size of the wash basket. Compact capacity runs 1.7 to 2.3 cubic feet; medium is 2.1 to 2.5 cubic feet; large is 2.7 to 3 cubic feet; and extra large is 3.1 or more cubic feet. Families with children and several loads daily may like the convenience of a large-capacity washer. Smaller-capacity models, which use less water and energy, can be economical for singles and couples. Front-load washers use less water, making them energy- and environment-friendly.

Wash and rinse speeds, temperatures, and cycles Basic washers have between one and four agitation and spin speeds. Some top-of-the-line models offer additional options. Preset wash cycles combine differing speeds, temperatures, and levels of agitation to clean specific types of clothing. An average washer may have regular, permanent press, and delicate cycles. High-end models may offer additional cycles, such as a heavy-duty cycle for work clothes, jeans, and towels, as well as presoak and prewash cycles for dealing with difficult stains. Water temperature options usually include hot/cold, warm/cold, and cold/cold. Some more expensive models feature additional temperature combinations to suit more fabrics. Controls are mechanical, with rotary knobs and push buttons, or electronic with conveniences such as digital displays and more custom cycles. Water-saver options recycle water from lightly soiled loads.

High-efficiency (water- and energy-saving) washers Save energy and extend the life of your clothes and linens with a well-designed washing machine. For energy efficiency, look for models with the Energy Star designation. Consider horizontal-axis, front-loading washers or top-loading washers that tumble instead of agitating clothes. These models use less water and energy than top-loaders of the same size. They use the same amount of detergent as regular washers. The amount of detergent needed depends on the load size, not on the amount of water used. Front-loading washers are ideal for washing linens without going out of balance. Consider the following additional features:

★ Delayed starts, common on dishwashers, allow you to turn on the washing machine when utility rates are lower.

★ Automatic water level control selects the right amount of water for each load to prevent overfilling.

★ Internal water heaters reduce demand on your home water heater.

★ Polypropylene and stainless-steel washtubs don't chip or rust as enameled steel can. Smooth interior surfaces are easier on clothes.

★ Spin speeds of 700 to 1,600 revolutions per minute mean that clothes are almost dry when they leave the washer. Drying gets done in less time and at lower temperatures.

Selecting a Dryer

Consider energy costs as well as basic and special features when you purchase a clothes dryer.

Capacity The size of the dryer drum determines capacity, which is measured in cubic feet. A larger capacity means the dryer is capable of drying more clothes. Descriptive terminology varies according to manufacturer, so check the actual cubic-foot capacity when shopping for a dryer. In general, dryer capacity ranges include compact (2 to 4 cubic feet), medium (4 to 5.8 cubic feet), large (5.9 to 6.9 cubic feet), and extra large (7 or more cubic feet).

Cycles, temperatures, and controls Basic dryers include delicate, permanent press, and regular cycles. Expensive models offer more options for fabric care. Some models include a cycle for home dry-cleaning products. Standard temperature settings are hot, warm, and cool; some moderately priced dryers include timers and settings for specific fabric types.

Labor-saving dryers Minimum drying times save energy and reduce wrinkling. To iron as little as possible, use the lowest dryer setting and do not overdry. Remove laundry as soon as the dryer stops. Take out all-cotton and permanent-press clothing when slightly damp and hang to dry. Consider other dryer options:

⭐ Electronic moisture control detects moisture content to prevent overdrying and shrinking.

⭐ Dryness monitor indicates a nearly dry load; minimizes ironing.

⭐ A damp-dry cycle shortens drying time; garments can be ironed while damp or finish drying naturally, which is better for knits.

⭐ Two-direction tumbling keeps clothes from clumping as they dry.

⭐ An interior dryer-drum light helps to locate small items.

⭐ A stationary rack allows shoes to be dried without tumbling.

⭐ Time-remainder indicators give readouts of the time left in cycle.

Washer-Dryer Combinations

These efficient appliances, designed for small spaces, are available in stacked, side-by-side, or all-in-one units. Before selecting one of these styles, consider where the combo will be located, such as in a closet or in an upstairs bedroom or bath. Selection criteria are the same as for standard washers and dryers.

Speed Clean Your Way Through That Laundry Pile

Follow These Tips for Washday Success

Sort light colors from dark colors. If you have doubts about the colorfastness of an item, wash it separately in a low-water setting, or in a minibasket if your machine has one. To check for colorfastness, mix a small amount of detergent with a cup of water. Moisten a seam or inconspicuous spot. Rub with a clean, dry white towel. If color comes off, the garment should be laundered separately.

Check pockets for pens, crayons, coins, tissues, and anything else you and your family put into pockets. Be especially vigilant if you have young children who put crayons in their pockets. If the crayons survive the wash, they will surely melt in the dryer. Many orange-oil cleaners can remove crayon stains.

Treat stains and heavy soiling before washing. Pretreat shirt collars and cuffs that are heavily soiled using a prewash stain removal product or liquid laundry detergent. For very tough stains, like blood, try ice cold water first. Hydrogen peroxide works great for blood stains that have dried on a fabric. Never put stained items in the dryer. If the stain remains after laundering, re-treat with the stain removal product and rewash.

Use the recommended detergent amount; for heavily soiled garments, large loads, or hard water, use a little extra. Excess laundry detergent will not get your clothes cleaner. Instead, it could leave a filmy residue or discolor bright garments.

Check the water temperature, especially in the winter. Detergents work best in warm or hot water. Use cold water only for washing clothes that might fade or clothes that are lightly soiled.

Wash delicates in mild detergents made for fine washables, such as knits and sweaters. Turn delicates inside out and use the delicate or knit setting. If you machine-wash delicate blouses, pantyhose, tights, or lingerie, place them in zippered net bags.

Never overload the washer or the dryer. In the washing machine, tub capacity and load weight determine wash-cycle water levels. Putting too many items in the machine leaves less room for water, so circulation decreases, limiting effective cleaning. A too-heavy load also can damage fabrics as they rub against the agitator. "Walking" washing machines that shift out of position and go noisily off balance during spin cycles are often caused by overloading. Consistent overloading can bend the washer's frame or damage the motor, which eventually requires repair or replacement. The consequences of overloading the dryer are equally dire. Overloading results in poor air flow, so it takes more time and energy to dry clothing and linens. Too many overweight loads can result in misalignments of the drying drum, necessitating repair.

Proper washing machine loading: Check the loading instructions on the machine's lid. If these are not available, the most common order is detergent, laundry items, and water. This prevents excessive sudsing and minimizes the risk of fabric damage from full-strength detergents directly in contact with clothing.

Dryer loading: Underloading can be as wasteful and inefficient as overloading. Overloading prolongs drying time and can result in uneven drying; too few items in the load doesn't use heat efficiently. Either use a short cycle to avoid overheating a light load or wait until you can dry more items. Avoid putting heavy, hard-to-dry items in the same load with lightweight items.

Drying times depend on load size, garment weight, and fiber content. Six cotton bath towels that weigh 5 pounds will dry in 40 to 50 minutes, for example. A permanent-press load of 12 items—slacks, shirts, shorts, and dresses—also weighing 5 pounds, will dry in 30 to 40 minutes. As load size increases, so does drying time. If the dryer seems to run for a long time, it may be the final cool-down cycle, which minimizes wrinkling. Some dryers offer extra tumbling without heat. One of my favorite dryers has a two-hour wrinkle-guard cycle.

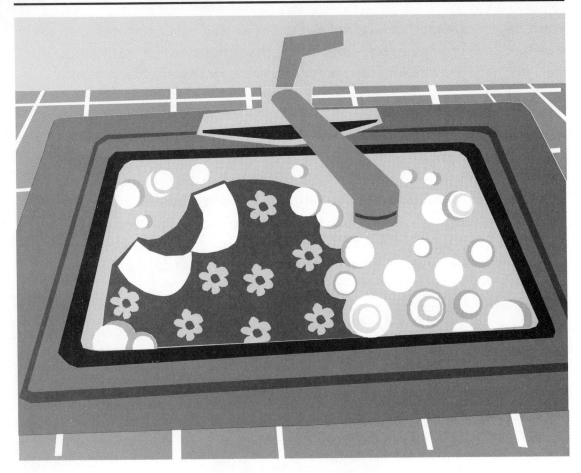

Hand-Wash Laundry

Read care labels for instructions and water temperature. I know many of us hate to read labels, but as expensive as clothing is, it's important. Some clothing, such as cotton knits and sweaters, retains color and shape best when hand laundered. For best results, use a mild laundry detergent or product made for hand washables. Products with high alkaline content are not recommended for cotton hand washables. Read the label to be sure.

Fill a sink or small tub with water and detergent. Soak the garment; never scrub or twist. Rinse with clear water. Gently squeeze out excess water. Don't wring. Roll heavy garments in clean cotton towels to remove water. Use a towel that has been laundered several times so there's no lint to cling to the newly washed garment. Follow label directions for reshaping and drying your garment.

Stain Removal

Protect your investment in washable clothing and linens by promptly and correctly treating stains. If a fabric is dry-clean-only, blot off excess stain and take the garment to the cleaners as soon as possible. Always point out stains and spots so they can be marked for special professional cleaning. The following tips are for general home laundry.

Photocopy this list and post it in your laundry room or near your washing machine and dryer. As a general rule, inspect all clothing and linens. Treat stains as soon as possible and pretreat before washing. If a stained item goes through the drying cycle, the stain will be harder to remove.

Baby formula Pretreat or soak stains with a product containing enzymes. Soak dried stains for at least 30 minutes. Launder normally. (Always launder infants' clothing in mild detergent formulated for baby clothes.)

Blood For fresh stains, soak in cold water (hot water sets stains). Launder. For dried stains, pretreat or soak in warm water with a product containing enzymes (read the label). Launder. If stain remains, use a bleach safe for the fabric.

Chocolate Pretreat or prewash in warm water with a product containing enzymes. Or treat with a prewash stain remover. Launder. If stain remains, rewash with bleach safe for the fabric.

Collar and cuff soil Pretreat with a prewash stain remover, liquid laundry detergent, or a paste of granular detergent and water.

Crayon For a few spots, scrape off the excess with a dull knife. Place the stained area between clean paper towels and press with a warm iron. Replace paper towels as the crayon is absorbed. Place stained area facedown on several layers of clean paper towels. Sponge with a prewash stain remover or cleaning fluid. Blot with paper towels. Allow to dry before laundering. If color remains, rewash with chlorine bleach, if safe for fabrics. Otherwise, use a color-safe bleach. For an entire load of clothes affected by crayons loose in the dryer, wash with hot water using laundry detergent and 1 cup of baking soda. If color remains, launder with chlorine bleach, if safe for fabrics. Otherwise, pretreat or soak in a product containing enzymes or a color-safe bleach. Use the hottest water safe for the fabric and rewash.

Diesel fuel or gasoline Use extra caution when treating these stains—they can make clothing flammable. When washing fuel- or gasoline-soaked fabrics, use only detergent-based stain removers, not solvent-based ones. Air clothing and other items thoroughly and do not place in the dryer if fuel smell is detected.

Fruit juices Soak in cold water (hot water sets the stain). Wash with bleach safe for the fabric.

Grass If lightly stained, pretreat with stain remover or liquid laundry detergent. Launder using hottest water safe for fabric. For heavy grass stains, place facedown on several layers of paper towels. Apply cleaning fluid to the back of the stain. Replace paper towels as the stain is absorbed. Let dry; rinse. Launder using hottest water safe for fabric.

Ink Some common inks are extremely difficult or impossible to remove. Common inks include ballpoint, felt-tip, and liquid. Try one of these three pretreatments before giving up. As the easiest first step, pretreat with a prewash stain remover and launder as usual. Don't put in dryer if stain remains. Instead, try another method. Using denatured alcohol, hair spray, or cleaning fluid is a method worth trying. Sponge the area around the stain with one of them before applying the solvent to the stain. Place the stain facedown on clean paper towels. Apply alcohol, hair spray, or cleaning fluid to the back of the stain, frequently replacing the paper towels. Rinse thoroughly; launder. As an alternative method, place the stained fabric over the mouth of a jar or glass. Hold the fabric taut so the ink spot doesn't spread. Drip the alcohol, hair spray, or cleaning fluid through the stained fabric; as it leaves the fabric, the ink will drop into the container. Rinse thoroughly with cool water; launder as usual.

Mustard Pretreat with stain remover. Launder with chlorine bleach, if safe for the fabric, or with color-safe bleach.

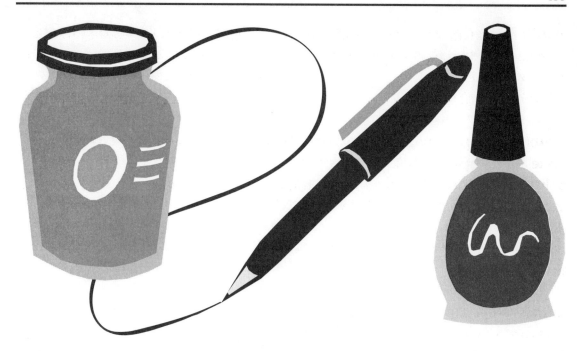

Nail polish This may be impossible to remove. Try this method using nail polish remover, but don't use on acetate or triacetate fabric. Place stain facedown on several layers of clean paper towels. Apply remover to the back of stain. Replace towels as they accept polish. Repeat if stain begins to lift. Rinse and launder.

Paint (water-based) Rinse fabric in warm water while stains are wet. Launder. For dried paint, take the article to a dry cleaner who may be able to remove the paint. Removal depends on the paint formulation and the fabric.

Paint (oil-based paint and varnish) If the label on the paint can recommends a thinner, use that solvent for stain removal. If the label is not available, try turpentine. Rinse. Pretreat with a prewash stain remover, bar soap, or laundry detergent. Rinse, launder, or take to a dry cleaner. Oil paint is more difficult to remove than latex.

Perspiration If perspiration changes fabric color, apply ammonia to fresh stains or white vinegar to old stains; rinse. Launder using hottest water safe for fabric or wash with an enzyme product or color-safe bleach in the hottest water safe for the fabric.

Scorch Fabric may be beyond repair. Launder using chlorine bleach, if safe for fabric. Otherwise, soak in color-safe bleach and hottest water safe for fabric, then launder.

Urine, vomit, mucus, feces Pretreat or soak in a product containing enzymes. Launder using chlorine bleach (which also disinfects), if safe for fabric. Otherwise, use color-safe bleach.

Stain Removal Tips

★ **Blot rather than rub to treat a stain.** Blotting draws the stain away from the fabric; rubbing pushes the stain into the fabric and damages the fiber, finish, and color of the fabric. Use a gentle rubbing motion under running water to help remove dried food, protein, or oil stains from denim-weight fabrics of cotton or cotton/polyester blends.

★ **Use white, lint-free towels.** Do not use terry cloth or dark-color cloths when blotting; lint and dye transfer worsen the problem.

★ **Check for stains.** Pretreat before washing.

★ **Check that the stain is gone** before putting wet laundry into the dryer. If the stain persists, do not put the item in the dryer. The heat of the dryer can make a stain permanent.

★ **Wash heavily stained items separately** to avoid transferring stains.

★ **Do not use hot water on stains of unknown origin.** Hot water can set protein stains in the fabric.

★ **Never wash pesticide-soiled clothes with other laundry.** It can contaminate the entire load.

Products to Stock

Keep the following products on hand. Note that all products should be kept on upper shelves or in locked upper cabinets out of the reach of children. Never leave any of these product packages on the washing machine; drips could damage machine surfaces. (See Laura's Favorite Products, p. 188–189).

- ★ Non-sudsing household ammonia
- ★ Chlorine bleach
- ★ Color-safe bleach
- ★ Color remover
- ★ Commercial stain removers
- ★ Mild hand-dishwashing detergent for hand-washing
- ★ Dry cleaning fluid or petroleum-based pretreatment solvent
- ★ Paint remover
- ★ Petroleum jelly
- ★ Rust removers
- ★ Prewash spot remover and towelettes
- ★ White vinegar

Common Laundry Problems

Grayness, overall Causes are insufficient amount of detergent, low water temperature, or incorrect sorting. Increase the amount of detergent, use a detergent booster or bleach, or increase wash temperature. Sort heavily soiled from lightly soiled items and carefully sort by color.

Grayness, uneven Usually caused by insufficient amount of detergent, low water temperature, or improper sorting. Sort garments by color and rewash with an increased amount of detergent and hottest water safe for the fabric.

Yellowing May be caused by buildup of body soil. Increase the amount of detergent; use a product with detergent booster or bleach safe for the fabric, or try both methods at once.

Blue stains Detergent or fabric softener may not be dissolving or dispersing. If detergent causes the problem, soak the garment in a plastic container using a solution of 1 cup white vinegar to 1 quart water for one hour, rinse, and launder. If you have been using fabric softener, rub stains with bar soap. Rinse and launder. To prevent stains, add the detergent and turn on the washer before adding laundry. If using fabric softener, dilute the fabric softener in water before adding to wash or rinse cycle or to dispenser.

Powder residue Usually caused by undissolved detergent. Always add detergent before filling tub and adding laundry.

Stiffness or fading May be caused by hard water. Use liquid laundry detergent or add a water softener to granular detergent.

Lint Caused by mixing items that give off lint, such as bath towels and napped velour or corduroy fabrics. Wash such items separately or with like fabrics. A clogged washer lint filter or full dryer lint screen may be the culprit. Tissues left in pockets also cause this problem. Check pockets before washing and check washer filter frequently. Clean the dryer lint screen after every load.

Pilling This is a wear problem and a characteristic of some synthetic and permanent-press fabrics. If necessary, use a lint brush, or a tape or gel roller, to remove pills. Adding a fabric softener in the washer or dryer may also help. When ironing, use spray starch or fabric finish on collars and cuffs. Use a medium setting to avoid scorching delicate synthetic fabrics.

Shrinking Avoid the problem by following care instructions on labels. Shrinkage is irreversible. Reduce drying time and remove garments when they are slightly damp, This is especially important for cotton knits.

CHAPTER EIGHT

Organization

We have spent a great deal of time in this book working on getting your home clean in half the time. To keep your home looking its best, we have to keep in mind that cleaning and organizing are two separate tasks. You can be well organized but still struggle with keeping the house clean; or you can be a perfect housecleaner but disorganization makes your home look a wreck. Help is here: Call this Speed Organizing 101!

In chapter one, we discussed visual cleaning. You can spend all day scrubbing and sterilizing your home to a hospital standard, but if you have clutter your home will look dirty. In this chapter, you will learn some of the simplest ways to get your home organized and keep it that way.

For years I have I have admired rooms pictured in books and magazines that feature closet organizers, baskets, garage organizers, pantry shelving, and sliding kitchen drawer trays. Who doesn't dream of having a place for everything and everything in its place? It's easy to declutter and organize your furnishings and possessions. The difficulty is in finding the time and the willpower to let go of unneeded possessions.

True Cleaning Confessions

I know a woman who suffers from respiratory problems. Years ago, I helped her clean her home. Once a week we cleaned until her house was spotless! Each time, we cleaned objects most people would only do periodically. We would vacuum her CD player, radios, furniture, and draperies. We used cotton swabs to clean the carved crevices on her dining room chair backs, which collect dust. She also had an air-purifying system that did a great job of keeping the dust level under control. You could not find a speck of dust in her house. The problem? Disorganization. She had cleaning under control but needed help in getting organized. We assessed her clutter hot spots and were able to find a solution for each one. There are tools on the market that make getting organized easier than it ever has been. My friend felt overwhelmed for so long that she let me use her story as an example to help others. This chapter will teach you how to apply the lessons we learned to your home.

> **TIP** Get organized. Every household chore is easier when your home is well-organized and relatively clutter-free. When you have to declutter before cleaning or cooking, even small tasks seem monumental.

STEP 1 Schedule an organizing day. Make organizing a priority by making an appointment with yourself. Schedule it on your calendar, handheld organizer, or day planner. At first, you may only be able to find just a few hours. In that case, attack one room. If you are drowning in clutter to the point that your home looks like an indoor garage sale, you may need help.

STEP 2 Ask your most organized friend(s) to help you. Many of cable TV's popular organizational shows require that an unbiased third party help. You can get the same honest advice from friends, who can help you through the denial, sentiment or nostalgia, and withdrawal stages of organizing your home. Being a pack rat can account for 90 percent of our clutter! This chapter will make decluttering a painless experience.

STEP 3 Review your clutter hot spots. This will help you create a workable, reasonable plan. Set priorities, then systematically get to work, room by room and closet by closet. Allow extra time if you are dealing with notorious out-of-sight areas such as attics, basements, and garages. Set a realistic goal of clearing one room per week or one room every two weeks, depending on your time and possessions. If you want quicker results, block out one hour each day, go on strike with your other obligations for a day, or recruit outside help. Whatever you do, don't stress over organizing. Move at your own pace.

STEP 4 Tackle problem areas. Put safety first and deal with fire or safety hazards. These include improperly stored flammable items, such as paints, solvents, oily rags, and gasoline—even a stack of old newspapers is a potential problem. Once you've dealt with safety issues, move on to the area that bothers you the most or the one your spouse keeps hinting about!

STEP 5 Sort your possessions. Many professional organizers recommend that you divide items into one of four boxes: trash, sell, donate, or sentimental favorites. Clearly label containers and fill them. Then you'll need to store the keepers. At a superstore, I bought several see-through plastic tubs with lids for $2 each. Then I bought heavy-duty plastic shelving and created storage space in my basement and garage for less than $50. There are flat bins on wheels that fit under beds, and over-the-door racks and accessory pockets for closets. If the space under your beds or at the backs of closets is limited, you can find other workable storage solutions. Even the attic holds more than you can imagine.

STEP 6 Practice the one-year rule. If you have not used something in a year, chances are you don't need it.

STEP 7 Hold a garage sale. As you sort, clear, and organize, prepare for a garage sale (if you have the time and energy to pull off that amazing feat!). Designate a holding area, such as a corner of your basement or a closet shelf or two. Wash and neatly fold items. Keep masking tape and markers in the designated area. Price and identify each item before you store it. When the garage sale weekend arrives, you'll have a big task out of the way.

STEP 8 Donate to charity or give to a family in need. Declutter and do a good deed. Donate clothing and household items to a charitable organization. Check to see if the organization will pick up large items, such as furniture. As an added benefit, items donated to charitable organizations may be tax-deductible. Keep a list of your donations, the condition of each item, and your receipt from the organization. If the item is valuable, take a snapshot or a digital photograph for your records. If you have questions about what and how much is deductible, check with your tax preparer or the Internal Revenue Service. For more information on charitable deductions, visit the IRS website at *www.irs.gov.*

STEP 9 If all else fails, hire a professional. If your time is limited and you have the money, get a grip on organization by hiring a professional. A professional organizer can offer advice and services tailored to you and your family. Areas normally covered are space and storage planning, managing paper, and busting clutter. Find a professional organizer in your area through the National Association of Professional Organizers at *www.napo.net.* Franchise or locally owned closet component firms also may offer space planning and storage advice along with installation.

True Cleaning Confessions

I learned young that one person's garbage is another's treasure. Mom taught all seven of us to get the most out of every gift or hand-me-down. A scarf, pair of shoes, or toy can light up the face of a child or an adult in need. The joy of giving outweighs the pack-rat syndrome and can be an inherited family trait. Little did I know my 17-year-old daughter had watched my giving through the years and inherited the desire to give to others. In high school, she volunteered at a food pantry where families posted wish lists. My daughter asked me if she could give one family its wish-list items from things we didn't need: two bikes (we had six), a computer (we had two new and two old ones), board games (we had 10), a portable boom box (we had four). She called the family, and the mother and her three children were outside waiting for my daughter to drive up. My daughter told me that the smiles on the children's faces, and the way they excitedly ran up to the car, filled her with joy. When you donate your possessions you may never see who gets them. I can guarantee the families who receive your treasures are grateful.

Room-by-Room Organizing

Here's how you can find and create storage space, sometimes in unexpected places, throughout your home.

FRONT ENTRY

This is the first peek visitors have into your home. While the goal is an attractive, uncluttered, functioning space, how it is set up depends on your residence and family. If you buy or build a house, don't overlook the convenience of a coat closet near the front door. Don't allow this important part of your home to be even a temporary dumping ground. If your family primarily uses a side or back door, mail and packages may be the main front-entry organizing issues. If this is the entry everyone uses, or if you live in an apartment or a condominium with only one door to the outside, you'll need an aggressive corralling and controlling strategy. Realistically assess how much stuff enters and leaves your home through this area. Think about how long items need to be in the entry area before they can be stored. Also consider seasonal concerns. Because this is an entry from the outdoors, cold-weather and rain gear, such as coats, boots, slickers, and umbrellas, may need to be stored nearby. In a snowy locale, a bench where you can take off or put on boots, with nearby storage for boots, gloves, and hats, prevents tracking slush and outerwear through the house.

> **TIP** Control incoming and outgoing mail, keys, and small packages with a hall chest. Find a style—from traditional to contemporary—and a size that fits your space. Use the top drawer or a tray on the top for mail. If the family primarily uses this entry, school papers, books and tapes to be returned to the library or video rental store, and other transit items can be stored neatly in the chest.

Quick Fixes

★ No room for a chest? Hang a shelf for mail and keys. Have a local carpenter craft one to your specifications or check local retailers.

★ No coat closet? Install a coat rack and rotate seasonal coats and rain gear to avoid clutter. An umbrella stand is an old-fashioned convenience that serves a practical purpose.

FAMILY ENTRY

Depending on the layout of your home, you and your family may enter through a garage or carport, or a side or back door. Whether this is a back-stoop space or part of the porch or kitchen, the family entry has the potential of becoming the family dumping ground. Because guests rarely use this entry, it's tempting to let clutter pile up. Here are organizing ideas to control the stuff of life.

Consider how you and your family use the entry. Use the space to keep the household running smoothly. Many times I have referred to myself as an air traffic controller. My job is to safely move everyone in and out on time and with his or her personal belongings. The family entry gets the most wear and tear. Organize a space for items that are needed daily or frequently: Have a basket for school papers, hooks for backpacks and umbrellas, and shelves for briefcases. Pet owners find it convenient to keep leashes at this entry. Bottom line: The less unnecessary stuff you keep in this busy area, the better.

The family entry also stores rain and winter gear, such as slickers, hats, jackets, and boots. During the school year or special camp programs, sports equipment, book- and athletic bags, and lunch boxes typically pass through. Plan or redesign the family entry with built-ins. Designate one wall as a mini locker with a built-in unit for sports gear. Measure the sizes of key pieces of equipment, such as tennis rackets, baseball bats, and hockey sticks, and have shelves built to size. Purchase bins or buckets to corral smaller items, such as tennis balls and baseballs. Use this area for sports gear in active use. Organize out-of-season gear in the garage or basement.

TIP Allow a separate shelf or two, preferably with racks for drying, in the family entry area for dirty or muddy athletic shoes. If space permits, designate sections of the built-in for individual shelves or bins for each child or adult who plays a sport. A nearby bulletin board with a calendar is a convenient way to keep game and practice times where everyone can see them.

Quick Fix

★ If you or your child needs a place to pull off boots or change from athletic shoes, add built-in seating with handy sports storage. With a simple plywood addition, perhaps crafted as a window seat with a hinged lid, you'll have a place to neatly stash gear. Apply a tough enamel paint to stand up to daily life. Or purchase a sturdy unfinished chest and add racks and bins inside for shoes or gear. Purchase a heavy-duty wide bench and add bins below the seat to keep gear handy and out of family foot traffic.

MUDROOM

The name says it all. Mudrooms were originally designed to keep farmyard mud out of the house. There's still a good reason to designate such a space.

Once a common feature of country houses, mudrooms are a practical way to keep your house clean—especially if you live in a climate with months of wet or snowy weather. In traditional farmhouse design, the mudroom was the working entry from the outdoors. In current design, country or country-style houses may have a combination mudroom and laundry or potting area. A small bathroom, with a shower or at least a sink, may be included. If space is tight, a mudroom can be an expanded back-entry area with storage for outdoor gear and a place to change and store shoes and boots and leave soiled outdoor clothing. Shelves, racks, and hooks and pegs provide storage. In some climates, your concern may be dust and dirt or winter salt and sand from the city streets. If boot or shoe storage is only seasonal, consider placing shoe or boot racks in the mudroom.

Creating a new mudroom. Decide what you need before you plan your mudroom. Do you live in the country and have outdoor animals, or do you garden much of the year? Do you work in an occupation that requires you to clean up or store gear? Do you walk to work or walk from the bus stop or train and need a neat place to leave your boots and coat to dry? Do your children play a variety of outdoor sports? Will you combine your mudroom with another function, such as doubling as laundry room? Will a small bath or a sink for washing up be included in the plan? Each situation demands its own storage solutions.

LIVING ROOM

Whether you call this area a living room, family room, or great room, the furnishings in this space are what make your residence a home. How do you organize and store family photographs, books, magazines, travel souvenirs, collections, musical instruments, electronic gear, and perhaps toys and games? Consider the type of living area you have. Do you have the traditional formal living room plus a family room or den? Does it function as a single room, or is it a combination living area and dining room? Whatever the type of space, how do you use it?

FORMAL LIVING ROOM

In homes with two or more living areas, the living room is usually used for conversation and entertaining rather than active family living. Storage is based on appearance and style rather than strictly utilitarian concerns. Some home styles, such as the bungalow, feature built-in shelves flanking the fireplace. Current home styles may include a small living room off the entry that doubles as a library. The addition of built-in bookshelves may be all it takes to convert a room into a dual-purpose library and formal sitting room. To add interest to a living room, paint the backs of the built-ins a dramatic color, such as red. If your budget allows, have the built-ins constructed with base cabinets that complement the room's woodwork for concealed storage. This can be an ideal solution if you want a television or other electronic equipment in the room.

FAMILY ROOM OR DEN

Second only to the kitchen in family activity, the family room has its own unique organization and storage needs. In open plans, the family room is usually part of the kitchen and close to a secondary entry. Whether that entry is a mudroom or a side or back door, clutter in the area must be controlled to preserve the appearance and function of the family's main living space. Because this is where the family lives, the daily clutter of life—such as newspapers, magazines, mail, books, hobbies, projects, videos, and perhaps the computer—can take over. If clutter is a problem for your family, hone in on their activities and plan your storage accordingly. The position of the television in the living room or den—tucked away or open and visible—dictates how much storage is open and how much is concealed. For many families, built-ins, wall-mounted bookshelves, or bookcases with bins or baskets are requirements for keeping things under control. If children use the family room as a play area, a toy box and bins for blocks and other small items are essential. Large sturdy baskets for toys and books are another option. Window seats also add accessible storage.

GREAT-ROOM

This combination room offers challenges and opportunities for organization. Because the space is open and visible, plan for concealed storage as well as open shelving. Built-in seating with storage can expand your options in the dining and living areas of a great-room. If built-ins aren't practical in your situation, purchase freestanding storage units that offer a combination of open shelves and concealed storage. For additional concealed storage, use trunks or ottomans with hinged lids. Arrange baskets or bins inside these pieces to keep small items or craft supplies neat and organized. If you like a vintage look, shop for a bookrack and accent table combination that can add chair-side storage. Plan built-ins for electronic and computer equipment or purchase storage units geared to your needs. Computer cabinets designed to resemble armoires when closed are practical in the open spaces of a great-room.

Musical Instruments

These valuable pieces deserve special care in your organization plan. Your piano will hold its tune much longer if it is placed against an interior wall. This instrument is sensitive to overnight temperature swings through an outside wall. Pianos also need humidity. If the air in your home is dry from the climate or from indoor heating, compensate with a combination humidifier-sensor attachment available for pianos. (Check with a piano dealer for a source and proper installation.)

If you own brass, wind, or string instruments, keep them in their cases, which may have humidifier and sensor attachments. (If your instrument is old, check out the possibilities of a new case for safer storage.) If you are storing an instrument for use in years to come, such as an older child's band instrument for a younger sibling, store it in a climate-controlled part of your home, never an unheated attic or dank basement.

Remove all tuning slides and valves from brass instruments, such as trumpets and tubas, then wrap each piece in tissue paper or cloth. Don't use plastic because it retains moisture. Remove the reeds of a clarinet, oboe, and other woodwind instruments. For stringed instruments, such as violins and cellos, turn the keys to release the pressure on the strings and store the instruments in their cases, fitted with a humidifier and sensor to prevent cracking.

Entertainment and Electronics

Adapt vintage, secondhand, or reproduction wardrobes or armoires as television cabinets. Measure your television, including the depth, before shopping for such a piece. Some storage pieces are too shallow to hold a television. Normally, the back of the unit will have to be drilled or cut for wiring, and will need well-supported shelves added. These units are usually large enough to also house a DVD player and discs, or a video cassette recorder and tapes. It may also accommodate a CD player or stereo unit.

A butler's tray is a classic solution for working a bar into a living room. If you use a butler's tray, pour liquors or sherry into decanters. Vintage tea carts on wheels or vintage or reproduction metal utility carts also serve the purpose.

Quick Fixes

★ **Install floor-to-ceiling metal shelving tracks** on one or more walls in your family room or den. Have $^3/_4$-inch-thick, 10- to 12-inch-deep plywood planks cut to fit, and hang them from adjustable brackets. Support the shelves at least every 24 inches to prevent sagging. Use stock molding and other stock detailing to trim basic built-ins or freestanding storage pieces. Look for detailing at home centers and at specialty woodworking shops that carry reproduction trim, often based on 19th- and early 20th-century styles.

★ **Fit shelves to the slope of a vaulted ceiling.** Use the centered wall space above the door for display. Build sturdy shelves for heavy collectibles. Use $^3/_4$-inch plywood and reinforce it with edging strips. Vary heights and widths to accommodate your collectibles.

★ **Check access to electrical outlets and wiring boxes** before anchoring shelves to the wall. Be certain you have the number of outlets and electrical boxes you need now and in the future.

★ **Divide shelving into groups of three.** An odd number is more visually pleasing than an even number.

★ **Think beyond the obvious** for storage and display. Look at a variety of pieces, such as metal baker's racks, for shelving options.

Space Savers

★ Hang a painting, print, or photograph from a vertical bookcase support for prominent display. The piece immediately takes on importance and conserves valuable wall space.

★ Buy your display pieces ready-made and painted or stained. Accessory and decorating shops and home decorating catalogs sell shelves and brackets, including ledges for art and framed photography. Measure spaces and order to fit. Stack several shelves for the display you need. Shop for a ready-made wall-mounted cabinet or a hanging corner cupboard. These are ideal for organizing a collection of small objects.

★ Turn a closet into a library by removing the door, replacing the trim, and adding interior shelves. Measure a love seat or sofa and have shelves built on either side for a recessed nook.

★ House a television in a cabinet to create a room divider between open living and dining areas. Maximize use of the space by incorporating bench seating with storage into the room divider. Have the bench crafted so the top lifts for magazines, videocassettes, table linens, or other items you like to keep handy.

★ Even rooms with 8-foot ceilings have enough space for a bookshelf over the door. The same idea can work with wide-cased openings if you reinforce the spans every 24 inches. Have shelving built from floor to ceiling on the unbroken wall in a small den to create a library effect. Add handsome boxes or baskets with tops for concealed storage. Buy matching boxes or baskets in identical or in graduated sizes. If you save magazines, purchase specially sized containers for a neat appearance.

Quick Fixes

★ Add a pair of étagères (freestanding open shelves) to a living room to display collectibles.

★ Convert baskets or trunks into cocktail or coffee tables. Inside, store seasonal throws. If space is extremely limited, use trunks, vintage suitcases, or baskets on stands as side tables. Use the interiors to store games.

★ If reading material takes over your living areas, add one or more magazine racks. Purchase large flat baskets to store newspapers. Clear out newspapers daily and magazines every week or two. Keep magazines in specially designed storage units or stack them on shelves—stacks of design or travel magazines can be attractive on the lower shelf of a bookcase. Or purchase European-style metal magazine bins that attach to the wall. Make books and magazines part of the decor by neatly stacking oversized books to serve as small tables; keep coasters nearby to protect your books.

★ Use the space under a skirted particleboard table to temporarily declutter a room. Purchase tables, such as glass-top patio tables, that include shelf-style bases. Place a console table behind a sofa or against the wall and add squared wicker baskets or trunks with tops. Install a shelf around the perimeter of your room for basket or bin storage.

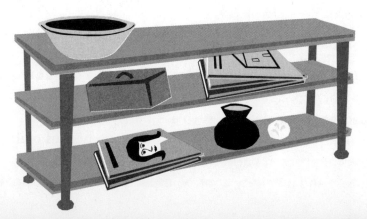

DINING ROOM

Whether your home has one dining area or both formal and informal dining spaces, storage in or near the dining area is the key to organization and function. Built-ins can be customized to your needs, but freestanding wardrobes, cupboards, and armoires adapt well and can add style to your setting. If you use some items, such as holiday china or serving pieces, only occasionally, consider storing them elsewhere. This will free valuable space for the dinnerware and glasses you use frequently. If you entertain during holidays only, a bar cart may work better than keeping a bar set up year-around.

Space Savers

★ **Turn an interior wall of your dining room into a sideboard** by installing floor-to-ceiling cabinets. Use the top cabinet to store little-used or seasonal items, such as holiday decorations. This arrangement provides much-needed storage in houses built without basements or attics. It's also better than garage storage for temperature and humidity control, especially in damp climates.

★ **Build cabinets and open shelves around the window** in a small dining room. Include a wine rack. Find room for built-ins by using space between wall studs. This shallow storage works for glasses and plate display. Fit a compact corner cupboard into a small dining area. Look for vintage pieces or paint or stain an unfinished one. Use the top for display or plants that need little light.

Quick Fixes

★ **Maximize storage and function** with a built-in sideboard or server for china, flatware, linens, and serving pieces. Measure your plates, trays, and serving pieces for a custom fit. Add a built-in china cabinet with glass doors on both sides to define a dining area without blocking light.

★ **Take advantage of the counter** between the kitchen and dining room in an informal dining area by attaching glass shelves with metal supports. Glass keeps the look open and adds display. If you have curved wood shelves, common in homes built in the 1940s and 1950s, replace them with glass.

★ **Consider something other than a matching dining room suite.** You can often get better buys on antique, vintage, reproduction, or contemporary sideboards sold separately. If stained pieces aren't compatible, prime and paint the sideboard or detail with a decorative paint finish. Look for pieces that are compatible in scale and style. Use a narrow console table, such as a metal and glass piece, for a server in a small dining area. This type of piece takes up much less space than a conventional sideboard.

★ **Let your dining room do double duty.** If you are a collector or have a home library, have floor-to-ceiling bookshelves installed on one or more walls of your dining room. Have shelves built around cased openings and flanking windows to create a library or museum ambiance.

★ **Replace solid doors with glass-paned ones to update an old server.** Have an old sideboard refinished with a combination of colors and finishes and updated hardware. Replace pulls on a built-in or freestanding server; look at some of the fun motifs on the market or mix plain pulls of different colors.

★ **Create a server with storage.** Combine two metal or sturdy wood wine racks with a glass or painted plywood top. Place away from direct sun to avoid damage to your wine. Purchase a commercial serving stand from a restaurant supply company and top with a decorative tray for a server.

★ **Make a sideboard server** by skirting a plywood base and having a plywood top cut to fit. Use a heavy cloth, such as tightly woven linen, for pleats or gathers. Take advantage of the space underneath—with baskets, a wicker trunk, or stackable plastic bins or boxes—for extra out-of-sight storage. For organizing, buy a pair of stacked, pullout vinyl bins on stands and place them underneath to organize linens and serving pieces.

BUTLER'S PANTRY

Traditionally the butler's pantry is a small room between the dining room and kitchen used for storing china, silver, glassware, serving pieces, and linens. This arrangement works well for families who entertain and need extra storage and serving pieces. However, many of the convenient organizing ideas of the traditional butler's pantry also can be incorporated into informal dining areas. Although storage in a butler's pantry is often custom-built, stock pieces, such as plate and glass organizers and lazy Susans, can turn a closet or even a sideboard into your own version of this handy pantry. Before you plan a butler's pantry, determine exactly what you want to store. A combination of open and concealed storage provides accessibility and a convenient way to store more utilitarian objects. If you are beginning to set up a household, plan storage space for future serving pieces, such as large trays and coffeemakers.

Pantry Pointers

★ Fit stock under-the-counter cabinets with easy-slide drawer glides and wood dividers sized to your china. (Check with a kitchen cabinet firm.) Put stock plastic or wire dividers into drawers, and line them with antitarnish cloth if you store silver pieces there. If you use easy-drawer glides for bar storage, reinforce the drawers to support the weight of liquor bottles.

★ Keep tablecloths, runners, place mats, and napkins neat and unwrinkled with a pullout unit constructed from oversize wooden dowels mounted inside a frame.

★ Adapt storage to specific needs. Have an upper shelf custom made for stemware storage or install tracks (available at hardware stores) on the underside of a shelf. Use dowels from a home center or lumber store for vertical plate storage. Such cabinets often are open on both sides for easy access.

Space Savers

★ Construct your own butler's pantry by building shelving around a window in a back hall, laundry room, or kitchen. Choose adjustable shelves so you can store items of various heights.

★ If you have a closet in your dining room or nearby in a hall or kitchen, use the space for a butler's pantry. Purchase plastic stacking bins for dishes and glasses and hang tracks under shelves for wine glasses. Install hooks for cups and mugs. Use flat, lined baskets for stainless flatware. If you have silver or silver plate, store it in a chest to avoid tarnishing. Purchase foldout racks to hang table linens on the back of the door. Use the top shelf for large serving pieces, such as chafing dishes, or items that you use infrequently, such as coffee carafes and punch bowls.

KITCHEN

Storage is the key to how well your kitchen functions. No other room in the house is more storage-oriented. How much and what kind of storage you need depends on the size of your family, how much you cook, your lifestyle, and your cooking style. Most superstores and home-organizing stores have a selection of kitchen gadgets that will make you the envy of all of your neighbors. For only $5, I purchased a packet holder that grips my spice packets, chili mixes, rice bags, and powdered drink packets. I then bought $3 white wire shelves that I hang on the wall inside my pantry for spices. Plus, I bought plastic slots for inside kitchen cabinets, so I can place mail, kids' school papers, and bills in a safe place and keep my counters clutter-free.

Quick Fix

★ Add a baker's rack or cupboard to create a handy mini-butler's pantry. Shop for a baker's rack with wide lower shelves for a convenient serving counter.

Pantry Pointers

★ You can carve out a pantry from a sliver of wall space. When space is narrow but deep, fit the space with pullout shelving to put items at your fingertips; install shallow shelves between wall studs to store cans one row deep. You can also enhance your pantry storage space by purchasing a $5 rolling cart. I have one in my pantry, and I feel like a professional chef every time I pull it out.

★ Store rice, beans, flour, cornmeal, cereal, and dry staples in sealed see-through containers. You'll keep pests away and see supply levels. Use containers for small packets of sauce mixes that can get lost in the pantry. Squared containers are more space-efficient than round containers. Buy bag clips to keep snacks fresh.

Cabinets and Shelves

Consider options other than standard base cabinets. Standard cabinets are less expensive to build and install, but custom-made cabinets with both deep and shallow drawers may better organize kitchen items. Plates and bowls can be stored in drawers if you use dividers. Existing cabinets can be retrofitted with pullouts. Check with a local cabinet firm for options or hit those kitchen storage aisles. Pullout wire drawers that sit inside cabinets are incredibly popular. They provide easy access and organize products, dishes, or pans.

Space Savers

★ **Maximize work space** by keeping appliances that you use every day off the counter. I've found that storing my toaster, can opener, coffeepot, and other items in my kitchen cabinets makes my countertops look clean and organized. If you don't have enough cabinet space, buy the plastic three-drawer storage units on wheels. Hang utensils from wall-mounted hooks or pegboard, or group them in a pretty pitcher or vase and keep them on the counter.

★ **Install a counter-to-ceiling metal grid on a blank wall** Hang cookware and utensils from S-hooks. Remember, clear counters make your kitchen look clean and organized.

★ **Mount a narrow shelf on the backsplash** to keep salt and pepper, mugs, and frequently used items off the counter. Such storage might seem convenient for spices, but spices are better stored in a cabinet away from heat.

★ **Hang a shelf over a window** A metal-mesh shelf with S-hooks can hold items on its underside. Purchase a new or vintage hanging cabinet or corner cupboard for open storage in your kitchen. If an old piece has a timeworn finish, clean it up and enjoy the patina. Buy ready-made picture ledges, available from decorating shops and specialty catalogs, and have a frame shop rout grooves for plates. Hang them around your kitchen as plate racks.

Ideas That Work

★ For the ultimate in accessible storage, use open wall storage and open under-the-counter storage in place of conventional cabinets. Vary the heights of shelves or install adjustable shelves to expand your options. Use sturdy decorative baskets for items such as produce.

★ Retrofit existing base cabinets with pullout bins, racks, and lazy Susans for tight corners. Use baskets or color-coded plastic trays if you need to store easy-to-lose items. If you frequently use heavy kitchen equipment, such as a mixer or food processor, consider storing it on its own pullout and pull-up tray. Check with kitchen designers, custom dealers, or cabinetmakers for installation.

★ A standard base cabinet is normally sized to hold two recycling bins—an easy way to divide glass from plastic. For easy recycling, adapt one side with a pullout shelf and vinyl-coated racks.

⭐ If space allows, an antique or a reproduction dresser or dry sink adds kitchen display and handy concealed storage. Install cup hooks for a neat look. Home centers, discount stores, and shops specializing in organizing offer a wide selection of products.

Quick Fixes

⭐ Use drawer dividers for utensils instead of plastic organizers that quickly fill up with stuff. Visit a discount store, home center, or organizing specialty store to find ways to customize a kitchen. Add items such as lazy Susans to make corners accessible.

⭐ Find new uses for standard items. Stools, benches, and bookcases are ideal for attractive storage. Place a narrow table against a wall and arrange baskets underneath.

★ Products such as racks for glasses and hooks for cups and inside-the-door attachments utilize every bit of space.

★ Be neat and selective when concealed storage space is tight. As you buy cookware, collect only one or two types that display well together. This is more attractive than a hodgepodge of styles and materials. If you don't have a pantry, add shelves at the back of the kitchen door to store canned goods and seasonal items.

★ Compensate for minimal storage. Purchase a multitiered plate rack to keep everyday plates handy. Use acrylic or natural woven baskets with several compartments, such as those designed for buffets, to store frequently used flatware and napkins.

★ Tailor basket storage to your style. Use a chrome-plated steel basket with handles to keep fresh fruit neatly arranged, or store kitchen towels in a simple wire basket with wood handles. Collect baskets in one style and arrange on the top of cabinets—if space allows—to hold kitchen items, such as extra tools or napkins, when space is very tight.

BEDROOM

This is the most personal room of your home. Unless you constantly strive to be neat and tidy, it's easy to let down your guard and give in to clutter and chaos. When you get a handle on organization, however, you are on the way to creating a peaceful retreat. Normally a bedroom has at least a small closet, but beyond that, consider what you need and want for bedroom storage.

Take into account whether you have space for additional storage, whether you need to store seasonal clothing and bedding in the bedroom, and how many functions the room serves. Often, the bedroom also must function as a home office, study, library, computer room, or hobby room, so you'll also need to store paperwork.

Space Savers

★ Choose perforated clothes hampers that are too handsome to hide. They keep dirty clothes out of sight and organized for the laundry. Buy one for washable clothing and one for dry cleaning only. In a country- or cottage-style bedroom, use white wicker hampers to keep clothes for the laundry or cleaners. Shop antiques stores or flea markets for vintage hampers.

★ In a bedroom with little or no storage, use decorative storage cubes with lift-off lids as matching bedside tables or at the foot of the bed in place of a blanket chest. Specialty home decorating stores and catalogs carry variations of the versatile wood storage cube.

★ Use the space under a bed for heavy-duty plastic or cardboard storage boxes. (Purchase boxes with tight-fitting lids to keep out dust.) This space works well for out-of-season items, such as sweaters or blankets. Use it for belongings you don't need every day but that require climate control, such as photographs, books, and heirloom linens.

★ Skirt a particleboard table and use the space underneath for stacked boxes. Add a padded or wood bench and use the space underneath to stash out-of-season items in wicker suitcases or other decorative boxes. Purchase shoe racks for over the door or stackable shelves.

★ Take advantage of walls by installing floor-to-ceiling bookshelves.

★ Box-in windows with shelves above and window seats below to use every bit of space for storage and display.

★ Buy a bed with integral, under-the-mattress storage. Check with a full-service furniture store.

★ Get double duty out of your nightstand by placing a decorative box from an import store on a stand. Such decorative hinged boxes, which work well as lamp tables, are easy to access and handy for tissues, glasses, reading material, and miscellaneous clutter.

★ When you need maximum storage for items such as hats and bulky duvets or quilts, add a vintage or reproduction trunk or chest at the foot of the bed. Affordable wicker is easy to move.

TIP If space allows, use the most classic storage of all—the desk. Choose one with the drawer space you need. A small writing table can work if you need minimum storage for supplies.

CHILDREN'S ROOMS

Parents already know that children need lots of storage. Unless children have a playroom, the bedroom is the repository for their possessions. Teach your children from an early age not to store or leave toys, books, and school projects in the living or family rooms. The ages of your children are obvious factors, but also consider needs for schoolwork, projects, and hobbies. A small, low bookcase, storage cubes, and a toy box are sufficient for preschool-age children. When children enter elementary school, add shelves and a desk for basic school supplies. If your children have computers in their rooms, include storage for disks and games. When a room is shared, designate individual storage for each child.

Space Savers

★ Affordable stackable shelving is another great option for kids' toys. Children can move and return the toys easily, so you do not have to find toys or game pieces hidden under their beds. For higher-end organizing, work with a carpenter or cabinetmaker to design and build a twin-size platform bed with drawer storage underneath. Pullout drawers are safer than toy boxes because they don't have hinged lids that can pinch little fingers or trap young children inside. Drawers work well for older children's extra bedding, sweaters, sports equipment, projects, and collections.

★ You also can purchase a bed designed with storage. Check with stores that handle youth furniture. Consider modular furniture for a built-in look that's movable. Pair up storage pieces with a desk along a wall or in a closet. Incorporate a trunk on casters for clothes storage and a bedside table.

★ Install Shaker pegs or hooks near the bedroom door. To make and install a Shaker peg rack, cut a 1×3-inch pine board to length. Using wood glue, attach the board to the wall. Cut two pieces of $^1/_2$-inch-wide decorative molding the same length; nail them flush to the top and bottom of the board with finishing nails. Drill holes 5 inches apart for 3-inch-long Shaker pegs; glue pegs into holes.

Quick Fix

★ Some of the best shelving I have found for kids' rooms has come from garage sales. I paint it to match their rooms.

★ Build a low corner bookcase with smoothed edges for safe and accessible storage. Measure what you plan to store before you design and install shelves. Plan for adjustable sizes rather than standard symmetrical arrangements. Avoid sharp angles and corners that can hurt children. Consider weight loads. Architects often specify $3/4$-inch-thick birch plywood for bookshelves; spans should be no more than 30 to 36 inches between supports. If you use a thinner plywood, such as $1/2$-inch, reinforce it every 24 inches.

★ Children's bedrooms tend to be small; take advantage of every bit of space by building removable shelves in one end of the closet. Store everyday toys and games on low shelves.

★ Look at material alternatives. Economical painted particleboard, rather than laminate or birch plywood, works fine for built-ins.

★ Acquire storage pieces that can be used through the teen years, then placed in other rooms or settings. A dresser and an armoire that are ideal for baby clothes and diapers will work equally well for jeans and sweaters. Buy sturdy storage pieces that grow with children. Check construction warranties before you purchase child-size versions of office furniture.

★ As soon as children have homework, buy a desk with storage. As a budget-stretcher, shop for a vintage or an unfinished desk to paint. Standard desks are 30 inches high; computer stands are usually about 26 inches high.

★ Place the bed against the back of a freestanding wardrobe, making a walk-in dressing area behind the bed. If the piece isn't finished on the back, staple or glue fabric to cover rough edges.

★ For children in upper elementary or middle school, look for chests to paint and use for storage. Add plastic drawer dividers or stackable storage so items don't get lost in a deep chest.

★ Paint an unfinished chest or toy chest with blocks of color for color-coded organization. Make a sturdy desk from painted wood or metal filing cabinets. Paint or stain a 4-foot-long, 1-inch-thick wood plank or door that fits the depth of the cabinets.

★ Stack flea market suitcases to create a bedside or occasional table with storage. Buy sturdy large baskets, open or with tops, or large hampers for instant storage.

★ Purchase plastic crates to create a room divider with storage. Or stack and tie two pairs of crates so there is knee space between. Lay a plywood top with rounded corners, sanded smooth and painted, across the crate pairs to form a desk. Place heavy objects on the bottom for stability.

NURSERIES

You'll be surprised at how much storage your baby needs. The basics are a chest for clothes and a changing table with open shelves to keep supplies handy. As your baby grows, organize the closet with double rods for hanging clothes and add bookshelves and a toy chest. Center the crib on the wall and add matching storage units on either side for a built-in look. In a tiny nursery, borrow space from a closet by removing sliding or bifold doors. Add a smaller baker's rack for easily accessible storage. When space is really tight, purchase a small corner cupboard for extra storage. (Bolt it to the wall so it can't tip over.) Purchase a crib or changing table with integral storage underneath. Stretch your budget by purchasing a secondhand chest or dresser and painting it bright colors.

Quick Fixes

★ Buy a child-size coat rack to hang little outfits, or hang special dress-up outfits from a decorative Shaker peg rack. Hang a small display cabinet or decorative shelves or brackets on the wall. Install an expandable rack with pegs for little jackets, mittens, and caps.

CLOSETS

Closet space seems to be in perpetually short supply. This is especially true if you live in a pre-1960 house or apartment, both of which are notorious for small or nonexistent closets. If your closets are miserably small, add freestanding storage pieces, such as a wardrobe or an armoire, for hanging clothes. With planning and myriad organizing products, you can maximize the storage in every closet. Double rods for hanging shirts, slacks, blouses, and suits are a first step. This works well for children's closets too. Plan for special items, such as hats, that are easily crushed on closet shelves. Attach pegs, hooks, or racks to the insides of closet doors to make extra storage for hats, ties, scarves, and belts. Use hooks only for robes and belts because most clothing does not hang properly from hooks. The backs of closet doors also can hold racks or pouches for shoes and small items. If you can't hang double rods and still need more storage, utilize the space under hanging shirts or blouses with a low chest, a wicker hamper for out-of-season clothes, or stackable storage units. Add clear plastic bins in children's closets to organize toys without concealing them from view.

Space Savers

★ Get shoes, luggage, and other items off the floor. Use shoe racks, shelves, and hanging bags. Store little-used items, such as luggage, under the bed or in a utility area. Organize shelf space by stacking sweaters and storage boxes.

★ Organize your closet to streamline the morning routine. Group clothes by purpose—business and dress clothes together, casual together, crossover in the middle. Arrange by color and style for new outfits. Line up shoes by purpose and color; keep standbys where they are easy to find. Keep small items in a central spot; keep jewelry in a shallow drawer.

★ Maximize a walk-in closet by adding a small chest. Padded lingerie chests have traditionally been used in closets; any small chest will work as long as it fits the space.

★ Take advantage of the variety of styles of closet organizers. Ready-made vinyl-coated shelving units in various configurations are sturdy and economical. Look for racks or shelves that attach to closet walls or doors or try freestanding units.

★ Replace sliding closet doors, often found in houses built in the 1940s and 1950s, with easier-to-access bifold doors. Paint the doors to match the wood trim.

★ Turn a spare room into a walk-in closet. Fit it with bookshelves for folded items, double-hung rods for short items, and large shallow drawers for jewelry and scarves. Add a freestanding clothes rack on wheels if more storage is needed. Put in stacks of shoe shelves. Install a bank of built-in closets across a room wall.

★ Build shelving, drawers, or rod space into the dormer areas.

Quick Fix

★ Organize closet shelves with creative solutions such as reproductions of classic hat boxes. Look for thrift store boxes, small suitcases, or hat boxes. Place a comfortable chair near your closet to slip on shoes. Install decorative hooks to hang the day's clothes and a mirror to check your appearance.

★ If your bedroom closet is large, buy a cart for your portable television. Save bedroom floor space by rolling it out only when you want to watch it.

★ Remove your clothes from dry cleaner bags—humidity inside the bags can cause yellowing. Cedar blocks next to your clothes can have the same effect. Let your clothing air before hanging in the closet to allow body moisture to escape. The clothes will stay clean and fresh longer, require less dry cleaning, and last longer.

CEDAR CLOSETS

Cedar closets and chests can help protect your everyday clothing and textiles from insects and mildew. The cedar closet or chest must be tightly fitted, and clothing and textiles must be freshly laundered before storage. To make a cedar closet effective, eliminate airflow under the door and through electrical outlet covers, open screw holes, or holes made by hooks. Cedar chests are often a good choice because they can be fitted with tight sides and heavy lids.

Line a closet with cedar by placing the cedar over existing drywall or studs. Purchase $1/4$-inch tongue-and-groove boards or 4×8 panels featuring a cover of cedar chips. Panels are easy to install and budget-priced, and they boast as much fragrance as expensive boards. Don't use the cedar intended for decks; it doesn't have the same properties.

Leave the cedar panels or boards unfinished to enjoy the aroma. If the cedar loses its fragrance, sand lightly to restore. If the closet is in a perpetually damp place, find and solve the moisture problem. Common culprits include improper drainage around the house and improper appliance venting. Never attempt to cover damp walls with insulation and vapor barriers.

BATHS AND POWDER ROOMS

It's a rare bathroom that is equipped with ideal storage space for your particular needs and supplies. To get a fresh start on organizing, clear the bath of linens, lotions, tools, and medications that you no longer use. Nearly every surface and space can be used to boost your bath's storage space and efficiency—walls, doors, corners, and nooks. Consider how you use the bath. If a couple or several family members share the bath, designate shared and separate zones. If guests also use this bath, plan for storage that declutters and keeps the bath neat and presentable. Also keep in mind what items you store in the bath and how the space functions. For example, if this is your makeup and hairstyling area, you'll need storage for the various items you use.

Space Savers

★ Think shelves and more shelves. Add a shelf with brackets over the tub. If storage needs are great, add a second shelf over the door. Make every inch count with shallow shelves between wall studs. For extra storage when the medicine cabinet is overflowing, install a clear acrylic shelf on brackets above the sink. Use plastic canisters or small pieces of vintage or contemporary pottery.

★ For freestanding storage, add a small cupboard, chest, or corner étagère. If wall space allows, include a hanging cupboard or other decorative shelving unit.

★ Hang hooks for towels and robes. If you have children, hang hooks at heights that encourage children to hang robes and towels. Sew fabric loops on towels that young children use so that towels are easier to hang on hooks. Remember to hang a hook on the back of the door too. Metal hooks, in a variety of styles and finishes, give a sleek, updated look. A door-hinge towel rack also works well and doubles as a robe or clothing hook.

Ideas That Work

★ Skirt the sink vanity by sewing hook-and-loop tape to gathered fabric. For a lush look, measure the exposed sink with a tape measure and triple the measurement to determine yardage. Glue the loop attachment to the sink so that the skirt can be removed for laundering. Add a storage basket, wicker hamper, or stackable containers underneath for concealed storage. Never store cleaners or medicines in this under-the-sink area.

★ Convert a chest or small sideboard into a vanity and have a marble or granite top cut to fit. Or start with a self-rimming sink to keep the water off the original wood top. To be sure your project will work in an existing bath, consult a plumber and a skilled carpenter. The top drawers of a chest may have to be reshaped if you want to retain them for storage.

★ Install roll-out drawers—similar to those used in kitchen cabinetry—for deep storage at your fingertips. Mount racks on the inside of cabinet doors. Make a lower cabinet more convenient—remove doors and replace the shelf with a laundry bin.

★ Clear the countertops by using wall-mounted hooks or pegs topped with shelving for blow dryers or curling irons.

Quick Fixes

★ Declutter by boxing up the essentials that line the bath counter. A hair dryer can fit nicely in a decorative storage box. Use small boxes in complementary patterns and colors for easy-to-lose items, such as earrings and pins.

★ In a powder room, use a dough bowl, wood bowl, or pottery piece for guest towels. Metal or wicker baskets also work well for towels. Use a vintage dish for guest soaps or a small plate rack with decorative plates to hold guest soaps.

★ Turn bathroom essentials, such as cotton balls and cotton swabs, into decorative accessories by storing them in sturdy clear plastic canisters topped by metal lids, arranged on a tray for neat storage.

★ Add a small butler's tray on a stand for towels and other essentials. Turn a metal basket, such as a vintage egg basket with a handle from a flea market, into a decorative container for rolled towels or extra rolls of toilet tissue.

HOME OFFICES

Everyone needs an organized, dedicated home office. This can be a small nook used for paying bills and filing important papers or an entire room for a home-based business. The key to making the most of your space—however small or large—is paying attention to tasks. Consider a computer table or storage unit that folds out from a freestanding wardrobe or have a cabinetmaker convert a unit into your own mini office with sturdy, supported shelves. When you hang open shelving, take advantage of the space over windows and doors. Use collected baskets to organize supplies and papers, mixing sizes and styles to meet your storage and organizational needs.

Space Savers

★ **Include a built-in desk** with drawers and built-in bookshelves in your designated work space. Such an arrangement allows the family room, bedroom, or kitchen to double as an office.

★ **Install pull-out storage.** Have a cabinetmaker design and craft a vertical pullout storage cabinet for office storage. Include plywood organizing dividers, open bulletin boards, and a small bulletin board for notes and reminders.

★ **Transform a window nook into an office** with a pull-down, tambour-door built in (similar to the type used for rolltop desks). The door pulls down to conceal the computer and keyboard. Add file drawers below and, if space allows, floor-to-ceiling cabinets to keep papers and supplies out of sight.

★ **Install concealed storage.** Get the greatest value for your money with well-planned, creative, concealed storage. Have cabinets constructed as plywood storage cubes. Install doors that slide back and forward to conceal equipment and supplies.

★ **Choose freestanding office unit components** when built-ins don't meet your needs. Home-decorating catalogs, office furniture stores, home supply warehouses, and discount and home center stores sell units in a range of prices and styles. A local carpenter may be able to build a unit for your specific needs.

★ **Purchase affordable cube-style shelving units** from home furnishing stores or home product catalogs. Color-code by painting the interiors in a mix of your favorite vibrant colors. Add plastic bins and storage boxes from home organizing and discount stores. Use pottery, flowerpots, or decorative woven baskets to hold pens, pencils, and scissors.

Quick Fixes

★ **Organize desk drawers** with plastic divider trays or boxes to store pens, paper, paper clips, tape, and stamps. Use file folders to keep papers neat and organized.

★ **Make your own desk** with storage by using two contemporary-style filing cabinets to support a glass top. (Make sure the edges are beveled for safety.) Use files rather than piling papers on the desk top. Stack clear or colored bins for dust-free storage.

★ **Organize open storage** with matching metal record bins—available from shops and catalogs that specialize in storage solutions and from some discount stores. Substitute flat baskets for in- and out-boxes. Use larger baskets for mail, magazines, and projects. Add baskets with handles, including the divided baskets designed for buffet flatware.

★ **Conceal less-than-decorative items** on open shelves by storing them inside wicker attaché cases, baskets with tops, well-made picnic baskets, or vintage suitcases.

★ **Have fun with baskets, old and new.** As you visit crafts and antiques shows, shop for sturdy split oak or twig baskets made by folk artists or interesting Native American baskets.

★ **Use wicker trunks and bins to store larger items.** They are ideal under work counters or desks. Visit import or specialty gift stores for out-of-the-ordinary storage options. Footed boxes, stacked band boxes, and small leather trunks can neatly hold office supplies in style.

LAUNDRY ROOM

If you have a choice, floor plans with separate laundry rooms or combination laundry and mudrooms or hobby rooms are ideal for storage and organization. However, a corner of the kitchen or a closet can work well if you add organizing shelves on brackets or racks, and durable baskets. Remember the basics. You'll be dealing with dirty and clean clothes and with wet, damp, and dry clothes. Plan storage accordingly. Convert a closet into a laundry room with stackable storage units. Install racks for laundry supplies on the back of the closet door. If your washer and dryer are closed off by louvered bifold doors, install racks and deep shelves above the appliances for supplies and laundry baskets. Vinyl-coated mesh shelving units, available at stores that specialize in organizing products and at some discount stores, are economical and sturdy.

Quick Fixes

★ Install a closet rod for clothes that drip dry or that you hang directly from the dryer. Use double rods if you hang primarily shirts and slacks.

★ Add a rack for socks and similar items. Locate the rack as close to the washer as possible because socks notoriously disappear during washing.

★ Hang a sturdy shelf behind the washer and dryer for laundry supplies such as detergent and stain

★ If space allows, build in a counter for folding and sorting. Include open shelves for sorting bins.

★ Store an ironing board and iron in the laundry room. If the room doesn't have a storage closet, hang the ironing board from a heavy-duty storage hook. Add a utility shelf for items such as the iron and spray starch.

GUEST ROOMS AND MISCELLANEOUS AREAS

These are rooms that may house people only occasionally, but that can be useful for everyday organization. The trick is to do this attractively so guests don't know they're staying in a storeroom!

★ **Hang fabric panels** on wire line or a drapery rod suspended from the ceiling to add concealed storage in a room. Choose washable cotton fabrics that complement your decorating scheme.

★ **Add storage** to a traditional-style bedroom furnished with antiques. Shaker boxes in graduated sizes or wicker or wooden boxes hide necessities and clutter. Use an antique steamer trunk or wood trunk for blankets, pillows, and out-of-season clothing.

★ **Be creative with specialized storage.** Add wood, woven, or art-paper-clad decorative boxes to store papers, magazines, crafts projects, or mending supplies. Cover a plain cardboard box and its removable top with heavy gift paper, brown kraft paper, or colorful wallpaper scraps for affordable, attractive storage.

★ **Use the space on your dresser or the top of a chest.** Stack matching decorative boxes in graduated sizes to keep items such as earrings, costume jewelry, socks, tights, hose, or scarves handy for the morning rush. Control dresser-top clutter with colorful boxes in varying shapes, sizes, and materials to hold small pieces of jewelry.

★ **Create affordable dresser-top storage** with a lipped serving tray from a gift shop or import store. A flat basket serves the same purpose. If the bottom of the piece is rough, glue on felt squares to prevent scratching.

★ **Buy a freestanding clothes rack** and angle it in a corner behind an attractive screen if clothes are spilling out of your closet. Buy a new or vintage screen or make your own by hinging bifold doors from a home center and painting or covering them with wallpaper.

★ **Install hooks and pegs.** These classic solutions were used for storage long before closets. Hooks and pegs come in a variety of styles, sizes, materials, and finishes and work well in areas where convenience and visible storage are beneficial, such as near the back door.

★ **Try roll-out shelving.** Available at home centers and mass-market stores, this type of shelving comes in a range of widths and tiers. It works well for bringing items in the back to the front. If the load is light enough, a basket functions the same way. For long wear and service, look for well-made, smooth, plastic-coated metal shelving or heavy-duty plastic shelving. Colors typically are white, tan, or other neutrals.

ATTICS AND BASEMENTS

Your attic may have space to spare, but use it carefully. Heat and radical temperature swings make it unsuitable for many items. However, the attic is a fine place for storing items that aren't temperature-sensitive, such as holiday decorations, pottery, and housewares. Clothes, blankets, and linens can be stored for a single season. (If you don't have closet space for furs or leather clothing, store them at the cleaners.) Clean clothing and textiles before storage. If insects have been a problem in the past, spray attic baseboards with an all-purpose household insecticide. Fabrics need to breathe: Hang clothing and linens from a garment rack or rod hung from the rafters. Keep it dust-free by covering the rack with a clean cotton sheet. Store folded clothing in an acid-free cardboard box or one lined with a clean cotton sheet. Don't store clothing or textiles in plastic because moisture trapped inside can cause mildew. If you prefer, purchase garment bags designed for long-term clothing storage. If you have lots of clothing to store, purchase cardboard clothing boxes with hanging rods from moving companies.

TIP Don't risk storing valuable or heirloom clothing, such as a wedding gown, in an unfinished attic or basement. Wedding and christening gowns should be professionally cleaned and professionally packed. Store in a climate-controlled area, such as on a shelf of a bedroom closet.

Moisture is the chief storage concern in a basement. Mildew can be a particular problem in climates with long or hot and humid summers. Keep flooding or excess moisture at bay with a sump pump, floor drain, dehumidifier, or a combination of these. Check to make sure they are working properly. With precautions, an unfinished basement without ventilation, heating, and cooling can be used for items that are unaffected by moisture, such as extra dishes, pottery, glassware, hand tools, and plastic or metal toys.

My basement has more than 10 shelving units, each 6 feet tall, that house my seasonal decorations, party goods, old albums, photos, and more. I put everything in clear plastic storage tubs so I can see what I need without pulling anything off a shelf. My husband loves it.

OVERLOOKED STORAGE SPACE

Think you're out of room? Think again! It's likely that there are many places in your home that you can use for storage that you never considered possible.

★ **At your feet.** Build shallow drawers into the toe-kick space beneath base cabinets. Fitted with a touch-latch release, they can be opened with a tap of your toe.

★ **In the wall.** Carve out shallow display shelves between wall studs. This can be ideal for a kitchen or bath where many small items, such as spices or toiletries, are stored. Space flanking a fireplace also is a natural for storage.

★ **Behind the wall.** Cut a short stack of shelves, drawers, or a closet into a wall backed by unfinished space, such as attics or dormers.

★ **Under the stairs.** This sometimes-roomy space may be the most overlooked for home storage. Angled and deep, the space can be fitted with a series of pullout, pantry-style shelving units that will swallow books, files, sporting equipment, games, and more.

★ **Around a window or door.** Take advantage of this wall space to build maximum decorative shelving for books and collectibles. To avoid sagging shelves, use $3/4$-inch plywood and restrict spans to no more than 24 inches between vertical supports. Have the top of a window seat built with hinges for concealed storage. In a young child's room, sliding panels are a safer alternative to avoid pinched little fingers.

★ **Built-in banquette seating.** Include built-in seating in compact dining areas. Have seating built with open space underneath to store books or have doors installed to conceal items stored under the seat, or have seating built window-seat-style with hinged tops to store larger items.

Glossary

Now that you've learned the techniques of Speed Cleaning, it's time to become familiar with the terminology. These are terms you may come across either in reading this book or in dealing with a professional cleaning service.

Antibacterial Chemical formulated to kill harmful bacteria on surfaces.

Antiseptic Chemical formulated to kill viruses, harmful bacteria, spores, and fungi on living tissue.

Bacteria Single-cell organisms that come in thousands of species; many are beneficial. Harmful bacteria, however, cause disease.

Basic Cleaning Routine chores one must do on a regular basis to maintain a clean and sanitary home. This includes routine disinfection of kitchen and bathrooms, vacuuming, and dusting.

Cosmetic Cleaning Cleaning to restore, enhance, or repair items to look new again.

Disinfectant Chemical formulated to kill bacteria and some viruses on surfaces.

Dry Work Tasks that do not primarily require the use of water or liquid cleaners. These tasks include dusting, sweeping, and vacuuming.

Dwell Time The amount of time a product must remain on a surface to be effective. This is important when using sanitizers, disinfectants, or germicides.

Germicide An agent that destroys bacteria, viruses, and spores that carry disease.

HEPA High Efficiency Particulate Air filter. This type of filtration removes 99.97 percent of particulates 0.3 microns and larger, including mold spores, pollen, and fine dust.

High-Dusting Removing dust from areas above shoulder height. These areas include ceilings, walls, tops of tall furniture such as armoires, and door and window frames.

Lime Scale Buildup of alkaline residue from minerals in water that makes glass look chalky and gives chrome surfaces a dull gray appearance.

Low-Dusting Removing dust from areas below knee height. These areas include floors, baseboards, vents, and low furnishings such as foot stools.

Microfiber A soft non-abrasive material designed for use wet or dry for cleaning all surfaces. It electrostatically attracts dirt and dust, so it requires no chemicals or soaps.

Microfilter A filter that can screen out fine particulates.

Micron One-millionth of a meter, which is about $1/70$ the width of a human hair.

Mid-Dusting Removing dust from areas between shoulder and knee height. These areas include most furnishings, artwork and knickknacks.

Mildew Microorganisms whose spores become molds in a moist, warm environment; they feed on the substance on which they form and produce citric, gluconic, oxalic, or other organic acids that can damage paper, leather, cloth, and more. They also at times produce color that causes staining, which is difficult, and sometimes impossible, to remove.

Mildewcide A chemical additive that kills, prevents, or reduces mildew growth; often added to paints.

Mold A fungus that spreads by spores; it can develop on leather, cloth, paper, or other surfaces, especially in the presence of high heat and relative humidity. Its spores can trigger allergies.

Neutral A measure of pH that indicates a product is neither acid (low pH) or alkaline (high pH). Neutral cleaners are safe to use on waterproof surfaces.

Overclean Expending time and supplies on areas that don't require the effort; it contributes to the overuse of chemicals and can result in premature wear on furnishings.

Overspray Incorrect use of products that applies them beyond the dirty area; this can result in residue buildup and contributes to poor indoor air quality.

Particulate A mixture of solid particles and liquid droplets found in the air. Some particles are large enough to be seen as dust or dirt; others are so tiny they can be detected only with a powerful electron microscope.

Preventive Cleaning Proactive steps that prevent dirt buildup on surfaces.

RTU Ready to use.

Sanitizer A product that kills bacteria on living tissue (skin) or solid surfaces. Not all sanitizers include surface-cleaning products; check labels for details.

Speed Cleaning The ability to clean your home or office quickly and disinfect effectively while reducing cleaning time by 25 to 50 percent.

ULPA Ultra Low Penetration Air filter. This type of filter offers higher efficiency than a HEPA filter, measured by amounts captured rather than particle size.

Undercleaning Inefficient use of time and supplies, resulting in incomplete cleaning; increases future workload and contributes to problems such as the spread of bacteria, mold, or mildew.

Visual Cleaning An uncluttered, pleasant-smelling room appears to be clean—the room looks neat and clean to the eye.

Volatile Organic Compounds (VOCs) Chemicals that evaporate easily at room temperature. Organic indicates that the compounds contain carbon. Often, VOC exposures are associated with an odor, but this is not always the case. VOCs contribute to poor indoor air quality, and some can trigger allergies and serious illness.

Wet Work Tasks that primarily involve using water or other liquids. These include wet mopping and washing surfaces.

Laura's Favorite Products

Speed Cleaning means letting the tools and cleaning products do the bulk of the work for you. Here is a list of products along with Internet sites that provide purchasing information.

★ **Black Ostrich Feather Dusters** Genuine ostrich feathers pick up dust.

    www.texasfeathers.com/frame_homeprod.htm

★ **Cascade Shine Shield** A dishwasher detergent that protects dishes and glassware from etching is a household must.

    www.homemadesimple.com/cascade/products/base.shtml

★ **Ceiling Fan Brush** Attach this curved brush to a telescopic pole, reach the fan blades easily, and the job is done in minutes.

    www.ungerglobal.com

★ **Dirt grabber mat** One by every exterior door keeps floors and carpets clean.

    www.surfaceshields.com

★ **Hardwood Floor Care Products** Make your floors look new again!

    www.bonakemi.com

★ **Kaboom** Does the job on tough tasks, including removing soap scum.

    www.greatcleaners.com

★ **Lemon Oil** Good for so many things, it belongs in every cleaning kit.

    www.hollowayhouse.net

★ **Microfiber Cloths** A microfiber cloth cleans 90 percent of surfaces.

    www.bonakemi.com

★ **Orange Clean** This multipurpose orange-oil cleaner really does the job!

    www.greatcleaners.com

⭐ **Scrubbing Bubbles Fresh Brush** A toilet brush with a flushable pad with cleaner inside. It also is safe for septic tanks.
www.scrubbingbubbles.com/freshbrush.asp

⭐ **Shark Cordless Vacuum** This cordless vacuum cleans carpets, hardwood floors, and edges quickly and easily.
www.sharkvac.com

⭐ **Shark Portable Steam Cleaner** Sterilizes surfaces for a really clean home.
www.sharkvac.com

⭐ **Shark Transformer Vac** Powerful bagless stick vacuum carries its own tools.
www.sharkvac.com

⭐ **Sticky Critter** Use this washable gel roller to pick up pet hair, lint, and dust.
www.natlallergy.com/allergy/products/

⭐ **The Total Reach Duster** Lets you get into tight spaces—like under the fridge!
www.ungerglobal.com

⭐ **Ultramax Microfiber Flat Mop** A professional-style mop that cleans floors with star fibers that attract and hold dirt.
www.vileda.com

⭐ **The Unger Tele Pole** This handy telescopic pole lets you attach cleaning tools from dusters to lightbulb changers so you don't have to climb ladders.
www.ungerglobal.com

⭐ **Wright's Silver Cream** A cream cleanser that does more than polish the silver!
www.jawright.com

Index

A–B

Air quality, 29, 69, 70–72, 95
Allergies, 23, 70, 94, 95, 118, 119
Ambience, 33
Ammonia, 34, 35, 70, 71
Asthma, 23, 94, 95, 118
Attics, 183
Bacteria, 10, 77, 103, 106–107
Basements, 184
Basic cleaning, 22–25, 27, 109, 113, 117, 121
Bathrooms
  bacteria in, 106
  basic cleaning supplies, 109
  cleaning products for, 33
  cleaning steps, 109–111
  deep cleaning supplies, 109, 111
  organization in, 174–176
  preventive cleaning of, 41–43
  speed cleaning of, 25, 32–33, 89–93, 108–111
Bedding, 40, 118, 119
Bed-making, 14, 32
Bedrooms, 32, 117–119 164–166
Bleach, 34, 35, 70, 71, 125
Boundaries, cleaning, 14–20
Brooms, electric, 25
Butler's pantries, 158–159

C

Cabinets, 40, 103, 104, 105, 161
Caddies, cleaning, 34, 53, 89, 94
Carpet stains and dyeing, 39
Ceiling fan brushes, 10
Children and cleaning, 14–20, 32, 52, 53, 119
Children's rooms, 167–170
Cleaning boundaries, 14–20
Cleaning cloths, 81–83, 84, 90–92
Cleaning products
  basic, 73–74

  for bathrooms, 33, 42, 43
  for carpets, 39
  for floors, 104
  hazards of, 34, 35, 70, 71
  "home remedy," 65
  for kitchens, 102, 104
  for laundry room, 137
  neutral, 73
  over-spraying of, 11, 64, 90
  reading labels on, 34, 35, 64
  reducing number of, 69, 90
  specialist, 78–79
  techniques with, 11
Cleaning schedules, 23, 27
Cleaning standards, 14–18, 23
Cleaning terms, 12, 22–23, 27–31, 36, 41
Closets, 171–174
Clutter, 13, 14, 26, 32, 141, 142
Cosmetic cleaning, 36–40
Countertops, 40, 77, 102, 103, 107
Cutting boards, 77, 104, 106, 107

D

Daily cleaning, 12
Deep cleaning
  bathrooms, 109, 111
  bedrooms, 117, 119
  kitchens, 102, 104, 105
  living rooms, 113
  tasks, 28
  time required for, 27
Dens, 150
Dining rooms, 156–158
Dirt, 12–13, 23
Dishcloths, 106, 107
Dishes, cleaning, 25, 45
Dishwasher-rack repair kits, 40
Disinfectants, 25, 26, 64, 75, 103, 107
Drains, 106
Dresser tops, decluttering, 32
Drip pans, stove, 37

Dryers, 128–129, 131
Dryer safety tips, 123
Dry work, 94–99
Dusting, 24, 28, 41, 64, 84–85, 94, 118
Dust mites, 118, 119
Dust, organisms in, 70

E–G
Entrances, 12–13, 29, 145–147
Enzyme cleaners, 79, 116
Family rooms, 150
Faucets, 103, 106, 107
Floors
  bathroom, 111
  kitchen, 10, 11, 104
  preventive care of, 44
  restoring hardwood, 40
  speed cleaning spruce-up, 32, 33
  tile, 43
  time needed to clean, 10, 11, 33
  tools for, 10, 33
Foodborne illnesses, 107
Furniture, rejuvenating, 37, 40
Germicidal cleaners, 75
Glass cleaners, 25, 34, 35, 64, 74
Grease, 103, 105
Great-rooms, 150
Grout, 38, 43
Guest rooms, 181–182

H–L
Hand-washed laundry, 132
Handwashing, 76, 77
Hard-water deposits, 38, 103
Hardwood floors, restoring, 40
Healthy Housekeeper website, 7
High Efficiency Particulate Air (HEPA) vacuums,
  95–98
Home offices, 177–179
Kitchens
  cleaning steps, 102–104

  clutter in, 26
  deep cleaning of, 102, 104, 105
  floors, 10, 11, 104
  hot zones of bacteria in, 106–107
  organization in, 160–164
  speed cleaning of, 25, 101–107
  supplies for, 102
  time required to clean, 101
Laminate repair kits, 40
Laundry problems, 138–139
Laundry rooms, 121–132, 137, 180–181
Laundry, washing and drying, 130–131
Leather-repair kits, 40
Lightbulbs, cleaning, 110
Living rooms, 112–116, 149

M–O
Maid services, 22, 54–55
Mats, 12–13
Microfiber, 10, 24, 26, 33, 81–83, 90, 91
Microwave ovens, 45, 65
Mildew, 43, 79
Mold, 41, 42, 43
Mops, 10, 26, 33, 84, 91, 102
Motivation to clean, 47–57
Mudrooms, 148–149
Non-abrasive cream cleansers, 76
Nurseries, 170
Odors, 29, 79
Orange-oil cleaner, 74
Organization, 13, 14, 53, 60–61, 63–64, 141
  in attics, 183
  in basements, 184
  in bathrooms, 174–176
  in bedrooms, 164–166
  in children's rooms, 167–170
  in closets, 171–174
  in dining rooms, 156–158
  of entertainment and electronics, 152
  at entries, 145–147
  in family rooms or dens, 150

getting started, 142–143
in great-rooms, 150
in guest rooms, 181–182
in home offices, 177–179
in kitchens, 160–164
in laundry rooms, 180–181
in living rooms, 149
of magazines, 155
in mudrooms, 148–149
of musical instruments, 151
in nurseries, 170
overlooked storage space, 185
pantries, 158–159, 160
shelving, 153, 161
Ovens, 104, 105

P–S
Pantries, 158–159, 160
Porcelain sinks, 103
Pots and pans, 25
Preventive cleaning, 41–45
Refrigerators, 43, 103, 104, 105, 106
Rules for children, 19, 20
Sanitizers, 75, 76
Schedules, cleaning, 23, 27
Scratches, 39, 103, 104
Scrubbing tools, 25
Seasonal cleaning, 28
Showers, 38, 41, 110
Sinks, 45, 77, 103, 104, 106, 107
Soap scum, 42, 110
Specialist cleaning kit, 78–79
Speed cleaning
components of, 10–11
principles of, 60–62
Sponge mops, 10
Sponges, 76, 77, 106, 107
Spruce-up cleaning, 30–33
Stains, 39, 80, 103, 133–137
Standards, cleaning, 14–18, 23
Stove drip pans, 37

Supplies
for basic cleaning, 109, 113, 121
for bathrooms, 109, 111
cleaning caddies, 34, 53, 89
for deep cleaning, 102, 109, 113
for dry work, 94
for kitchens, 102
for living rooms, 113
organizing, 53
for wet work, 89

T–Z
Team cleaning, 66
Techniques, 11, 24–25, 60–62, 102
Time, 11, 27, 30–33, 54, 101
Toilets, 43, 92, 110
Tools, 10–11, 24–25, 53, 63–65, 84–87
Top-to-bottom cleaning, 61
Ultra Low Penetration Air (ULPA) filters, 96
Vacuuming, 25, 31, 94–99, 114–115, 118
Volatile Organic Compounds (VOCs), 70
Washers, 126–127, 129, 130–131
Water spots, on glasses, 40
Wave cleaning, 66–67
Wet work, 89–92
Whisk brooms, 114, 116
Window filters, 41
Wiping techniques, 11
Zone cleaning, 67